SYSTEMS
SELLING
STRATEGIES

SYSTEMS SELLING STRATEGIES

MACK HANAN

JAMES CRIBBIN

JACK DONIS

amacom

A DIVISION OF AMERICAN MANAGEMENT ASSOCIATIONS

Library of Congress Cataloging in Publication Data

Hanan, Mack.
   Systems selling strategies.

   Includes index.
   1. Selling. 2. System theory. I. Cribbin,
James J., joint author. II. Donis, Jack,
joint author. III. Title.
HF5438.25.H354   658.8'1   77-25034
ISBN 0-8144-5460-7

Seventh Printing

**To sellers of commodity products
and their managers**

*Who will at last be able to position themselves
    with true professionalism
As solvers of customer problems
    (not peddlers of parity products)
As managers of improved customer profit
    (not agile manipulators of price)
And instead of being dealt with as
    alternate suppliers, outside vendors,
    itinerants, mendicants, or worse,
Can become genuine partners with their
    Key customer accounts.*

Preface

There is nothing more vulnerable than a naked commodity product: naked to its customers and its competitors because it has been stripped of the unique performance benefits it once enjoyed. It is vulnerable to price erosion. Both customers and competitors try to drive its price down to the level of its cost, shearing its margins. It is vulnerable to substitution, either by similar products that have become virtual replicas and that also lack a distinctive performance advantage or by an alternate product that can fulfill a similar need. It is vulnerable to the greatest ignominy of all: losing a customer and acquiring a competitor in the same single stroke when a customer turns to self-manufacture.

Since it can no longer clothe itself in the mantle of uniquely advantageous performance, it must be able to add value to its users in other ways if it is to sell at all.

One way to add value, and it is the simplest and therefore the most popular of all, is to reduce price. The customer pays less for the same value. The value is thereby enhanced. A second way to add value is to maintain price but to give more in exchange for it. This can take the form of free premiums of many types, such as free goods, free services, beneficial terms and conditions, deals and discounts, and other concessions that would otherwise bear a price. The customer pays the same but receives a greater value.

We reject these two forms of price concessions as the only ways to sell all commodity products. For many commodities—more, we suspect, than we generally give credit for—there is a third way to add value that can also add to price. This third way is to cloak the commodity in a *system*.

A system is a package composed of a commodity product and one or more other products and related services. It is sold as a single unit whose price is based on the system's ability to add a unique value that the commodity product alone cannot offer. This value is the economic effect of solving a customer's cost problem by reducing the cost or solving a customer's revenue problem by increasing sales.

A commodity product that is packaged in a system undergoes a conversion. It takes on some of the most desirable selling attributes of branded products. For one thing, it can bear a premium price that is based on the total system's contribution to customer value, not the commodity product's cost. For another, it can be sold on the basis of the system's unique beneficial effects, not simply the commodity product's specifications, terms, and conditions. Third, a system can become proprietary, enabling it to establish customer preference as contrasted with mere acceptance, which is the best response that a commodity product can hope to generate by itself.

Systemizing a commodity product is, in effect, rebranding it. With rebranding comes the opportunity to recreate brand-type premium profits based on premium price. This is the genesis of growth. Systems selling is the best way—perhaps the only way in most cases—to increase the ongoing profit contribution of a commodity business.

Selling systems is different from selling commodity products. To sell a commodity, the seller must know the product, its technology, and its cost right down to the last mill. These areas of knowledge are all internal. The only things a seller must know about customers are their specifications, which must be met in order for vendors to be on their bid list, and their purchasing practices, policies, and people.

To sell systems, a seller must know a good deal more about a customer's business, especially in two key subject areas: (1) where major costs cluster in customer functions and processes that the seller's systems can affect, and (2) how a customer's ability to sell can be increased. The seller needs to know customer costs so that customer profit can be increased as a direct result of reducing these costs with a system. The seller needs to know customer sales potential so that customer profit can be increased as a direct result of installing a system. In short, selling systems requires knowing how to cause a significant beneficial effect and prove that it will occur in a customer's cost or revenue structure as a result of the sale.

A system is a way of selling commodity products that does not sell merely commodity products. Instead, it is the profit-improving effect of the system that contains these products that is offered for sale.

In the same way that a system is a package of products and services, systems selling strategies are also a package. As we originally began to assemble this strategy package of systems-selling skills so that we could help companies learn how to apply it, we discovered the key to systems selling that gives it its uniqueness and makes it work. *The sales representative is the key to selling systems.* He or she is a system's ultimate component.

Systems are better than commodity products for a seller to sell because systems can yield premium profits. Systems are better for a buyer to buy because systems can yield premium profit improvement. In both cases, the sales representative acts as the manager of an improved profit contribution. Our central belief, and the foundation of this book, which is designed to reflect it, can be simply stated in this way: There can be no greater motivating power in business than to release the business management thrust of a sales representative who can bring improved profit to both the home office and to customers. This is what systems selling does.

We have written *Systems Selling Strategies* as the third AMACOM book in a "system" devoted to the same central theme of improving selling profit by improving customer profit. In *Consultative Selling,* we have positioned the systems seller in the role of profit-improvement consultant who emphasizes the financial impact of the sales mission on a customer's business. In *Sales Negotiation Strategies,* we have set forth the basic win-win negotiation style and principles for a systems seller to use in conducting the type of consultative relationship we recommend.

Now, in *Systems Selling Strategies,* we are prescribing the systems concept as the means of solving comprehensive problems that would otherwise erode customer profit or keep it from being achieved at all. At the same time, we prescribe systems selling as the best means of improving a supplier's profit by enabling commodity products to command premium prices.

MACK HANAN
JAMES CRIBBIN
JACK DONIS

Contents

1

Perspective

In just three sentences a sales representative reveals whether he or she is selling a system.

In the first sentence, the systems seller identifies a customer problem in financial terms—that is, in terms of what the problem is costing the customer, or what the customer could be earning without the problem. If the seller mentions a product or service at this point, it is not a system sale.

In the second sentence, the systems seller quantifies a profit-improvement solution to the problem. If the seller mentions a product or service at this stage, it is not a system sale.

In the third sentence, the systems seller takes a position as manager of a problem-solving system and accepts single-source responsibility for its performance. In the course of defining the system in terms of the contribution its components make to improving customer profit, products and services are mentioned for the first time.

If a sales representative is selling a system, it is easy to predict what the fourth sentence must be. It will be a proposal of partnership in applying the system to solve the customer's problem.

A system's seller's problem-solving approach requires that customers be served by helping them improve their profit, not by persuading them to purchase products and services. To solve a customer's problem, a systems seller must first know the customer needs that underlie it. Only when a customer's needs are known can the expertise, hardware, and services that compose a system become useful components of their solutions. This distinction is the difference between servicing a product and servicing a customer. It enables the seller's customer relationships to be close, consultative, and long term rather than the simple sell-and-bill relationship that characterizes traditional customer-supplier transactions at the sales representative to purchasing agent or buyer level.

Positioning the Seller

What systems selling does, therefore, is to position the seller as the vital ingredient in the selling process. It has become necessary to do this in one industry after another—and to convert product sales representatives into systems sellers—because products and equipment have lost their premium value. Along with it, they have lost their value-based premium price. They have become commodities.

To remain profitable, many suppliers have come to the realization that they must sell something more than commodity products. Product-related services provide part of the answer. But the major contribution to conferring premium value on a customer, and hence the major justification for charging a premium price, is *added value*—the value that can be added to a commodity product by a system that is under the personal management of a systems seller who can apply it to solve customer problems.

In most industries today, the only thing that can be individualized is the seller's professional expertise in applying a system to solve a customer problem and in creating personal partnerships with customers so that a system can deliver its maximum benefits.

Products and equipment are undergoing increased standardization. Every supplier imitates every other supplier's "big winners" with only a marginal change here and there.

Even the hardware and software components of some systems are imitated by competitors. Uniqueness does not enjoy longevity. Sales representatives, as a consequence, are being progressively deprived of enduring product differentiation as a selling point.

Along with increasing product standardization caused by imitation, price erosion has also eaten away at product profit. More sales have been forced onto a price basis than ever before. Customers are saying to their sales representatives, "If you will not offer me premium value, I cannot offer you premium price." As a result, sales hinge on how big a deal can be cut, not how big a benefit can be delivered.

In addition to price reduction, it has become standard practice for customers to demand discounts in the form of increased free services. Many suppliers have found themselves in the untenable position of selling their product at or near cost and still being forced to give away services. Some of these services are necessary because customers are not able to make the most economical or effective use of complicated products without supplier help. In other cases, rapid turnover among customer personnel has often left the sales representative as the only source of continuity on a piece of business. The seller's experience has become invaluable to the customer. But no general format exists for a seller to be compensated for added services or know-how when a commodity product is sold.

Adopting a Service Mode to Sell a Product

Systems selling provides solutions to the problems of product standardization, price erosion, and the increasing demand for product-related services. There are several additional advantages. With systems selling, the seller acquires a far more interesting and profitable job. For one thing, there is the opportunity to make a larger sale because there is more to sell. Of necessity, the seller must also become involved more deeply in the operations of a customer's business and deal with a wider range of its buying influences and decision makers.

Systems selling also gives the seller a built-in opportunity to follow every sale with new sales that renovate and enlarge and modernize the original system. There is a natural continuity to the seller-buyer relationship created by systems selling that is totally lacking in most product-oriented sales relationships.

It may be that the principal benefit of systems selling is that it requires the seller to adopt a service mode in order to move products. The service mode forces on the seller a number of positive attributes. Service selling must be personalized and tailored to every individual customer. Service selling must be symbolized by a single seller who becomes the customer's consultant, not simply a vendor or alternate supplier. Service selling must translate the service into an economic benefit for the customer that makes an otherwise intangible service become tangible as a dollars and cents contribution to the customer's bottom-line profit.

Because of these advantages, systems selling has become the basic, day-by-day selling strategy in dozens of major industries: data processing, communications, materials cleaning and finishing, fire protection, personal and professional services, transportation, industrial manufacturing, environmental protection, construction, publishing, and packaged consumer products. By surrounding the core commodity product or service that is offered in these industries with complementary products and services, and then by positioning a sales representative as manager of the resulting system who will apply it in a way that improves customer profit, companies have overcome many of the problems of commodity selling—especially the prime problem of price erosion.

Signals to Sell Systems

Most suppliers come to the realization that their major money-making products have become commodities by the signals that their customers begin to send them. There are three basic customer signals that say: "You have a commodity, which you will have to sell on the customer's terms, not the supplier's.'' One signal is that the product is "too expensive." This means that its perceived value to a customer has fallen below its asking price. Value must therefore be added to the product in the form of a system in order to justify a premium price. Sometimes this first signal is expressed by calling the product "the same as the competition's." This means that its perceived differentiation has been standardized by competition. Distinctiveness must therefore be added to the product's system in the form of a unique profit-improvement benefit in order to raise its value and position it above competition.

A second signal is that the product requires "frequent service" or "sophisticated knowledge" to operate and maintain. This means that its added costs of operation, maintenance, and downtime are perceived to make the product's use uneconomical. Cost relief in the form of a maintenance contract and employee education program must therefore be packaged in a system with the product.

A third signal is that the product is subject to "rapid depreciation" or "technological obsolescence." This means that its value is perceived to dissipate so quickly over time that a desirable return on investment cannot be achieved. Added value over time must therefore be incorporated with the product in the form of a replacement and upgrading system that will keep it technically current and cost-effective.

Contributions to Customer Problem Solving

Customer problem solving is a user-oriented approach. It must be sold on the basis of how the customer is benefited, not according to the capabilities a seller possesses. Capabilities represent only potential energy. Benefits are actual energy applied to a customer. Customer problem solving has an intense you-type of focus. As an example of focusing capabilities on a broad range of customer problems, an environmental control systems seller might express its major contributions in the following manner.

1. *Relief from staff and resource diversion.* By bringing

our information resources and experience to bear for you, we begin at once to relieve your staff of many of the most complicated burdens of managing your "second business" of environmental control. One of our principal efforts will be to work with your operating people in engineering and general management functions. We will share our knowledge with them and help them incorporate our system into their accustomed procedures. In other aspects of our work, we will release you from the need to divert staff expertise from normal, income-producing activities onto highly detailed problems such as environmental equipment selection, negotiating with suppliers, or recruiting specialized talent. Nor will you be required to develop and maintain in house the information resources that are required to keep track of the broadening stream of economic, technical, and regulatory developments that can affect your operations.

2. *Relief from repetitive government contacts.* You will also be relieved of the need to make many of the repetitive and time-consuming contacts with environmental control agencies at all levels of government. If you find it advisable or necessary, we can help educate your people in this complex area.

3. *Relief from major capital investment.* You will not require a major capital investment. Thus you will be able to retain your operating funds and borrowing power. Or you can return them to income-producing activities. These benefits should yield obvious favorable effects on your cost of capital and your corporate return on investment.

4. *Relief from unpredictability of costs.* Your monthly service fee will be determined in advance. Your fee will reflect the services and hardware you require. With pollution control technologies and compliance legislation undergoing rapid important changes, your monthly service fee can provide you with two important hedges: one is against inflation; the other enables you to take advantage of upgrading your pollution control system at any time that new developments or requirements occur. If your operations undergo change over time, or if the legislative standards that affect them are altered, we will renegotiate with you the cost and components of any revised service package you may require.

5. *Relief from unreliability of system operation.* The total combined strength of all our capabilities that support your contract ensures the reliability of your pollution control system on a continuing basis. Your contract will define the precise nature and degree of the protection that is afforded by your system. Even further, it will specify the exact regulatory standards with which you will be in full compliance. In this way, the ongoing reliability of your control system will be assured.

Systems Selling Starts with Service

Systems selling begins with a service, not a sale. In this respect, it differs from product selling where service—often at a cost that is unrecoverable—follows a sale to sweeten its price. The service that precedes systems selling is customer needs analysis. When the needs for customer profit improvement have surfaced and been ranked in order of priority, a system can then be prescribed to meet them. The environmental control systems seller whose problem-solving approach we have just oriented to customer needs might headline its services-initiated approach in the following manner.

Phase 1. Needs analysis. In close cooperation with your top management staff, we will direct a confidential analytical survey of your operations to determine the extent to which you need to control air, water, or solid waste pollution. Your needs analysis will be carried out for you with one overriding objective—to establish the most technically feasible pollution control system that meets three criteria: (1) It must comply with all pertinent codes and requirements that affect you, (2) it must represent the most reliable system at minimum cost to serve your needs, and (3) it must fit the operating demands of your existing and planned facilities.

Our highly developed customer sensitivity has made us unusually alert to seeking alternatives that can deliver the highest reliability of protection at the least cost. In addition, our experience allows us to consider the widest range of options in designing a system that will fit readily into your method of operation. Our constant aim is to find "the best way" that

meets your cost and operating requirements and that will assure compliance.

In many cases, therefore, we may recommend a system to
provide particulate collection at the end of your process. In
other cases, we may find that the best way is to help you effect
a process change at the particulate's origin. Our resource
depth frees us from preconceptions and technical constraints
so that we may explore all feasible alternatives that can get the
job done.

Phase 2. System design, installation, and operation. We
will design, construct, and install a full-compliance pollution
control system. We will assemble for you the most cost-
effective equipment and put it into on-line operation. The
equipment mix that best meets your specifications may be ours
alone or it may include products of other suppliers. The overriding determinant is that your total system yields optimal performance for you.

In some cases, little or no equipment may be required.
Other cases may require special engineering. Often our experience in solving similar problems will enable us to recommend
standard equipment that is available on an "off the shelf"
basis, so that we can minimize your costs in dollars and time.
Whatever the nature of your eventual system, we will work
closely and in complete confidence with your operating staffs.
We will help them locate your system for you either entirely
within your manufacturing facilities or on a physically re-
moved off-plant site. We can furnish all equipment, materials,
and services. We can arrange to operate it for you by providing
the workforce, supervisory labor force, and the management
expertise you require. And we can thereafter revise or renovate your system to keep it continually in full compliance as
existing laws are upgraded and new laws emerge.

Phase 3. Service package. We will surround every equipment system we install with a total service package. A typical
package contains provision for routine machinery and replacement parts. It also includes a consultative information
and advisory service on economical operation procedures that
help ensure the reliability of your system as well as safeguard
its cost considerations.

We will also provide the mundane yet challenging service of keeping you up to date about changing regulations and new technologies that can affect you. We will be able to supply you with this information from the output of our own ongoing research and operating knowledge. Furthermore, in the normal course of our work, we will seek out marketable byproducts that can be derived from your emissions and effluents. We can also help you deal with all pollution control agencies that have an impact on your operations.

Phase 4. Service financing. We will manage the preparation of a financing plan through which you can pay for your environmental control system in the form of a monthly service fee. Our service fee becomes your method of financing pollution control. This fee recognizes that our essential contribution is to provide you with a comprehensive compliance system, not simply hardware. Under your plan, you may also arrange to buy your system.

In order to become properly positioned to sell systems, you must understand and accept the requirements of functioning professionally in an environment where products themselves are never sold and where systems are never sold on price.

We have identified 12 skill and knowledge areas that our experience suggests are the minimum daily requirements for converting from product selling to systems selling. The first requirement is obtaining the proper perspective.

In the following chapters of this book, we will set forth the remaining requirements. You will learn how to position yourself for systems selling and what preparation you must devote yourself to in order to accomplish two objectives: prepare to do the selling job and prepare to penetrate a customer's organization structure in a way that will create the partnerships you require in order to accomplish your mission.

You will also learn how to make a system prescription to solve a customer problem and how to package the system you prescribe so that it will be able to improve customer profit in the most cost-effective manner. Presenting your system, pricing it so that what the customer pays is translated into a return on investment instead of a cost, and protecting your system and its price from your customer's attempts to desystemize it are the next steps in your conversion process.

Finally, you will learn the added value of planning a system's ongoing growth, modernization, and eventual replacement with your customers. In this way, you will be able to maintain a close, continuing customer partnership that will help perpetuate the contribution you make to your own improved profit as well as that of your customers and your company.

2

Preparation

Preparation for systems selling begins with identification of the key customer accounts who are the best prospects for systems. These accounts form the seller's prime market because they are the principal source of profitable sales revenues. By pulling them out, the seller will have the highest-priority market segments pinpointed as major targets.

In every market, the "80–20 rule" will be found to prevail. This means that only about 20 percent of all customers will contribute to profit heavily enough for them to become key accounts. Yet these relatively few customers can contribute as much as 80 percent of the systems seller's profitable sales.

The 80–20 proportion is a generality. In some markets, it will require somewhat more than 20 percent of all customers to supply 80 percent of a seller's profitable volume. But in many markets, far less than 20 percent may account for 80 percent or even more of all profitable sales. Because of this, the 80–20 rule averages out.

Since the systems seller's key accounts will be those in the 20 percent category, the core of every systems business is obviously quite small. This is a sobering fact. Every key account is precious. To lose a key account is to lose lifeblood. The seller must become as important to every key customer as the customer is to the seller. Only when the seller becomes a customer's preferred problem solver can this happen. The seller must know more about key customer needs for maximizing process cost efficiency than anyone else. And the seller must be better able to apply problem-solving systems strategies to those processes than any other systems seller.

By definition, a key account is one of the 20 percent or so of all customers who will install the seller's most profitable systems and who will add to them and their utilization of them on a consistent, long-term basis.

In response to the systems seller's perceived superiority in understanding and serving its needs, every key customer account should be a potential purchaser or lessor of a complete or large-scale system. It may require multiple services, ranging from consumables to replacement components to consultation. It may periodically add new capabilities to the original system. It may acquire additional systems to complement or supplement its original installation. These activities do more than generate revenue for the seller. They enable the seller's profit on sales to be maximized by applying account knowledge in the most cost-effective way, milking the seller's familiarity with the account's process needs and trading fully on the climate of confidence the seller has created with the account's decision makers and influencers.

The Key Account/Key System Matrix

The 80–20 rule can be applied to target the key accounts and the key systems that will furnish a seller's major profitable sales volume from systems. To apply the 80–20 rule to potential systems accounts, the systems seller should ask the question:

Who are the 20 percent of my accounts that contribute three-quarters or more of my profitable sales volume, or could be persuaded to?

The names of the accounts that meet this criterion will provide the seller with a key account list.

To apply the 80–20 rule to systems, the seller should ask the question:

Which are the 20 percent of my systems that can be expected to contribute three-quarters or more of my profitable sales volume?

The names of the systems, along with their components that meet this criterion, will provide the seller with a key system list.

When a seller's key account list is matrixed with the key system list, as shown in Figure 1, a bird's-eye view of systems-selling opportunity can be seen.

Figure 1. Key account/key system matrix.

Key Accounts	Key Systems			
	System	System	System	System
1.				
2.				
3.				
4.				
5.				
6.				

Identifying Additional 20-Percenters

The systems seller has two jobs to do with regard to key accounts: maintain existing key customers and develop new ones. The additional 20-percenters represent future systems sales. They are developmental accounts. The seller should devote about one-fifth of total time to segmenting them out, evaluating their growth potential, identifying their needs and the profit contribution to be expected from serving them.

Identifying developmental accounts that can become key customers is the speculative portion of the systems seller's job. At least one prospective "big winner" account should always be under development. To do this, an average ratio of three potential key accounts will have to be worked up for every one that actually pays off. This is the normal ratio of success in new business development.

Where will a seller find the time for developmental work? It is not as difficult as it may seem. A monthly time budget of only 25 additional hours will provide 15 hours for key account developmental activities:

Total allocable hours/month:	175	200
1. Key account maintenance and follow-on	120	125
2. New key account developmental activity	35	50
3. Non-key account customer service	15	20
4. Administration	5	5

Preparing the Key Account Needs Base

For both key account maintenance and new account development, a vital part of the seller's preparation consists of gathering information on customer needs for systems. The seller's preparation is dependent on knowledge. And it is knowledge that the customer, and the customer alone, possesses. To learn it, the seller must gain the customer's participation.

In equipment selling, a sales representative very often makes a concerted effort to minimize the role a customer must play in order to complete the sale. The representative wants to make it easy for the customer to buy. An equipment representative may also believe, and be justified in doing so, that if greater participation by the customer is encouraged, hidden objectives will surface and demands will be encouraged for special considerations such as terms, deals, discounts, premiums, or the inclusion of customized features at standard price.

To sell systems, a seller must encourage key account participation in the selling process at a co-equal level of involvement. The most important information that a customer must be encouraged to communicate is the area of specific needs for benefits from a system. Unless the seller admits the customer into a partnership role in benefit-centering the sale, there is a predictably high risk of ending up with a dissatisfied customer. This will be true *even if the system works* in an operational sense. It will not be perceived as a workable system since the customer will not have participated fully enough in its specification.

The increased amount of customer participation that selling a system requires can be brought about naturally if the seller practices a policy of need seeking with a key customer's decision makers and influencers. This will help obtain *primary information* on customer needs. Direct knowledge of this type can then be supplemented as required by *secondary information,* which the customer can recommend or participate in helping obtain.

Obtaining Primary Participative Information

Primary information is personal, subjective, and immediate. It must be elicited from "the horse's mouth" of the key decision makers who will accept or reject the seller's systems and of their key influencers.

Figure 2 shows an audit for entering the names of an account's decision makers and influencers and the needs they express.

Obtaining Secondary Participative Information

Secondary information is published data that is available from private or public sources as supplementary background information to the primary information elicited from key customers. It is information that the customer's decision makers and influencers respect and will recommend to further round out the seller's knowledge of needs for process improvement.

Figure 2. Primary participation information audit.

Customer Name ————————————————— Industry Sic# ———

EXPRESSED NEEDS FOR PROCESS/FUNCTION IMPROVEMENT
BENEFITS

By Decision Makers	*By Influencers*
Name: —————————————	Name: —————————————
Needs Expressed	Needs Expressed
—————————————————	—————————————————
—————————————————	—————————————————
—————————————————	—————————————————
Name: —————————————	Name: —————————————
Needs Expressed	Needs Expressed
—————————————————	—————————————————
—————————————————	—————————————————
—————————————————	—————————————————

Standardized System Strategy for the 80-Percenters

The systems seller's emphasis on key accounts is necessary to ensure cost-effectiveness. It is the single most important strategy to maximize profit on sales. This is the reason why key accounts are key.

Yet not all of the seller's profitable sales volume will come from key accounts. If up to 80 percent of profit comes from 20 percent of accounts, then 20 percent of profit must come from the remaining 80 percent of accounts. This is good money. It need not be left on the table. But it will almost always be more expensive to earn since its sources are far less concentrated, their needs for individualized treatment may be considerably greater, and they may not offer the opportunity for the repeat, high-volume follow-on sales development that often characterizes key accounts.

For these reasons, the seller must create a different strategy in serving non-key accounts. To maximize profit, a mix of two strategies should be made.

One strategy is to create standardized, ready-to-install, off-the-shelf systems for the 80-percenters. In order to minimize consultative and installation costs, these standard systems can be sold or leased as commodities. As such, their price will include little or no prescriptive modification.

A second strategy is to accept custom-tailoring assignments from 80-percenters that depart from a standardized system's components or requirements but to assess a premium charge for customizing in order to cover the seller's added costs at a normal profit.

3

Positioning

The ideal positioning for a systems seller is *customer profit improver*. The seller achieves this position by affecting one or more of a customer's processes in two ways: reducing the contribution a process makes to cost or increasing the contribution a process makes to earning new sales revenues. A systems seller's primary identification with profit improvement rather than with products, equipment, services, or even with systems themselves gives the systems sales approach a decided economic cast. It focuses attention on the ultimate end benefit of systems, not their components or cost. This gives the seller the same profit-improvement objective as the customer. It also professionalizes the seller's mission by expressing it in business management terms, not sales talk. This gives the seller the same business language as the customer.

Because the systems seller's positioning is so thoroughly customer-oriented, the best way it can be made clear is by examining it from the customer's point of view.

Customer-oriented Positioning

If you were a customer doing business with a systems seller, you would be aware of that fact from your very first impression of the precise nature of the seller's principal business asset: an in-depth knowledge of one or more of your processes and how that knowledge can be applied to create the most cost-effective solutions to the operating problems they create for you.

The systems seller knows that your process problems often occur together in systems where one problem can cause or aggravate another. The seller's solutions are also based on systems. Each system will be a custom-tailored package of equipment and services. The equipment components of the system are its *hardware*. The services are its *software*. The seller sells the software and the hardware indirectly by proving to you the profit-improvement benefits of the entire system. This approach treats the entire system as if it were a service.

IN-DEPTH ANALYSIS

The systems seller begins to work with you by making an in-depth analysis of the process that is causing problems. In this way, the seller makes it clear to you that the systems business is a service business by beginning each sale with an "intangible."

In carrying out an analytical survey of your process, the systems seller will work in close cooperation with your process managers. Together, they will determine the true extent of the problems and agree on their nature. The seller's needs analysis has one overriding purpose: to establish the optimal solution in cost-benefit terms that will solve a problem. This means that the seller must search out the individual differences of your particular situation as well as factor in its broad similarities. In this way the eventual system to be prescribed will fit the operating characteristics of your processes with the highest cost efficiency.

OPTION SEEKING

The seller will impress you with an alertness in seeking options that can deliver the highest efficiency at the least cost. Because the seller represents a broad range of capabilities, several options can generally be considered in designing a system that will fit most readily into your methods of operation. The seller is under no obligation to advocate only a single cookbook solution. The sole preconception governing the seller's prescription is to find the solution that best meets your cost and operating requirements.

By bringing to bear a combination of personal expertise, experience, and information resources on your industry in general and your own business in particular, the seller begins at once to relieve you of many of the complicated burdens of improving the cost efficiency of one of your vital processes.

IMPLICIT PARTNERSHIP

The seller acts as an implicit partner. One principal aspect of partnership is the seller's work with your marketing, technical, and general managers. The seller shares knowledge of your problem and solution options with them and helps them incorporate the end solution into their operating procedures. If your process is subject to compliance legislation, the seller will also release you from the need to maintain your own in-house information center to keep track of the technical, economic, and regulatory developments that affect your operations. In other cases, the seller may also take on the responsibilities of actually operating your process or recruiting and educating your own people to do so. When required, the seller may also carry out negotiations on your behalf with other related suppliers to integrate their equipment into the system.

SUPPORT SERVICES

Once the seller knows your specific needs and has counseled with your operations managers on the most cost-effective solution for them, the seller will go to work and enlist support services to design, engineer, and install an optimal system. The seller will assemble the most cost-effective equipment and put it into on-line operation. Whenever standard equipment is available on an off-the-shelf basis, the seller will recommend it to you in order to minimize your costs in dollars and time.

The seller will surround the equipment in your system with services. A typical service package may contain provision for routine machinery inspection, repair and replacement parts and consumable supplies, service schools for your operating people, a consultative advisory service on the most economical operating procedures, and the application of new technological discoveries to your system as soon as they have been dependably commercialized. As an even further service, the seller may be able to help you find reusable and marketable byproducts that can be derived from the operation of your processes. The cost savings and income from these byproducts may help defray part of the system's cost.

FINANCING

The seller will probably be able to offer you the option of financing your system so that you can pay for it in the form of a monthly service fee. Either an installment plan approach to purchase or a continuing-lease method may be arranged. Whichever you prefer, financing can make your system afford-able without requiring you to undertake a major capital investment. Your operating funds can then be conserved or you can employ them in other ways. Your borrowing power can also be retained. These benefits can have favorable effects on your cost of capital and the rate of return you can receive on your system investment.

PROFIT IMPROVEMENT

The seller's principal asset is essentially operating savvy. The seller knows you have a business to run and works to help you keep it running while, at the same time, integrating the system into your operations in the most affordable, least disruptive manner that contributes most to improving your profit. The seller would like to be accepted as your partner in profit improvement. This is the basis for a long-term collaborative relationship with you during which you both will continually try to build onto the profit-improvement contribution of every system that is installed.

In all your dealings throughout your relationship, your seller will make it clear to you—by everything that is done as well as by everything that is said—that the most important component in every system is the *seller*. It is the seller's personal expertise that enables the seller to prescribe the optimal system to achieve your profit-improvement objectives. It is the seller's experience that insures you against the time and money costs of trial and error. And it is the seller's broad access to information resources, and the ability to apply that knowledge to solve your problems, that underwrite the cost efficiency of your partnership.

You can obtain the components of the system that the seller prescribes for you from alternate suppliers. Some may offer demonstrably higher technical quality. Others can prove demonstrably lower price. But none can offer you the *seller*. That is the ultimate source of your unique benefits.

Selling Return on Investment

As seen from the customer's point of view, the systems sales representative is positioned as an integral part of every system. Unlike a product salesperson who is identified as a part of his or her own company and therefore does not go along in the sale with its products or equipment, the systems seller is embedded in the system and is "packaged" along with it. While a piece of equipment may endure in relation to a customer's business for longer than the equipment seller, the systems seller—in contrast—generally goes on making an important contribution to customer profit long after the original system has been installed. The seller's durability with a customer aptly defines the vital role a seller plays over and above the other elements of a system.

A system sale is not the sale of products or equipment. Nor is it the sale of product-related services. It is not even the sale of the system itself. A system sale is the sale of a positive rate of return on the customer's investment: in short, the economic effect of the system. The ROI is contained in the system in much the same way that music is contained in an orchestra. It must be delivered by the systems seller, who orchestrates the system. The seller is the deliverer. For this reason, a systems seller is known by the ROI that is delivered.

Implicit in every system sale must be the assumption, held alike by seller and customer, that the system's return on investment is undeliverable without the seller. The seller's personal intervention is central. It begins with prescribing the system and flows through its delivery, installation, coming on stream, continuing maintenance, periodic upgrading, and eventual replacement. As long as the seller is perceived as the critical element, the system can hold together and resist being desystemized into separate selective purchases that are made on the basis of competitive price. The seller is the guardian of a system's premium price. If the seller is unable to deliver a return on investment that justifies a premium price, he or she ceases to represent the added value implied by the price premium, and the system may fall apart into its components.

In order to achieve a position as the single most important element in every system, a seller must acquire two skills which are over and above the typical skills of product sales. One of these skills is the ability to plan. Systems require careful planning, not only in their prescription but also in their presentation, installation, and ongoing operation. The second skill is the seller's ability to apply personal expertise to the knowledge resources of a customer's industry as the key to solving customer problems. These skills are usually associated with consultants.

Because the planning and applications skills are so important to systems selling, they give it the style and much of the substance of a consultant relationship.

To sell in a consultant manner, a systems seller will have to be able to achieve self-actualization through customer service. The seller will also have to learn and apply the principles of negotiation in order to consult with customers. Finally, the seller will have to install and operate a control procedure to monitor system performance so that it is always on plan and on budget in its delivery of the prescribed benefit.

Taking a Consultative Approach

A consultative approach to selling systems is service selling. When a product-centered or equipment-oriented sales representative makes the transition to systems, there are three guidelines that can help increase the newly required emphasis on service and away from product. These guidelines will affect the content of the seller's customer relationships in terms of what is sold, the style of the relationship in terms of how the sale takes place, and the value that is both *received* and *perceived* in the relationship.

1. *Increase the personalization* of the relationship. Equipment sales are based on performance of the equipment. Systems sales are based on the performance of the systems seller.

2. *Increase the customer's participation in the relationship.* Equipment sales are based on maximum sales representative participation and minimal customer participation. Systems sales are based on a high degree of active buyer–seller participation.

3. *Increase the professionalization of the relationship.* Equipment sales are based on a traditional buyer–seller relationship. Systems sales are based on positioning the buyer as a client and the seller as a consultant.

INCREASING PERSONALIZATION

A system cannot be separated from its seller. The seller endows systems with personality. Of all their components, the seller becomes their indispensable operating element.

The increased amount of personalization required by systems selling must be initiated by the seller in order to take leadership in the relation. The seller can become acknowledged by a customer as the system's leader only when the customer can perceive two truths about the way the seller performs:

1. The seller must personally become involved in understanding the customer's process for which a system will be recommended.

2. The seller must personally become involved in creating the customer's system, setting its profit-improvement objectives, and applying the system to achieve the objectives.

INCREASING CUSTOMER PARTICIPATION

Gaining acceptance as "process smart." The customer's process is the context for the seller's systems. It is therefore essential that the seller become "process smart" in the aspects of customer processes that will provide the basis for the successful creation, installation, and operation of systems. The seller must acquire this new knowledge firsthand, right on the customer's premises, with sleeves rolled up. Both literally and figuratively, the seller must be willing to get dirty hands by seeing the process and conducting give-and-take sessions with its operators, supervisors, and inspectors. There must be a demonstrated willingness to do this not just once but over and over again.

Increased personal involvement with the customer's process must be channeled in two directions if the seller is going to be seen as genuinely understanding a customer's business:

1. *Encouraging factual inputs* about the customer's process.
2. *Encouraging psychological inputs* about the customer's needs and expectation of benefits.

Encouraging factual inputs. A systems seller will probably never know as much as customers do about their processes. There is no need to. The seller must know more about systems that can solve process problems. To do this, facts are required about customer processes so that the seller can prescribe the most cost-efficient system and make recommendations for the composition of its service package. Figure 3 shows a factual input audit.

Encouraging psychological inputs. To be "process smart" means also to be "customer smart." Just as the seller is the vital component of every system, the customer is the vital component of every process. Encouraging customer participation by asking for factual inputs is therefore only one part of the story. The seller must also encourage the customer to

Figure 3. Factual input audit.

Factual inputs I must obtain in order to prescribe a system for
_____ to improve the profit contribution of its
(Customer Account Name)

_____

(Customer Process or Function)

CUSTOMER PERCEPTION OF THE PROBLEM TO BE SOLVED

_____
_____
_____
_____
_____
_____

CUSTOMER PERCEPTION OF SOLUTION

_____

Expected Contribution to Profit ($000)	Acceptable Contribution to Cost ($000)
$__ __,__ __ __	$__ __,__ __ __

_____

discuss the psychological factors that influence the way the customer perceives the process, its peculiarities of performance, and the nature of the problems that reflect its unique personality. The customer's perception of an ideal solution to the problems must also be sought. The seller's system will have to address itself to these issues and to solving the problems they give rise to. Figure 4 shows a psychological input audit.

INCREASING PROFESSIONALIZATION

The client–consultant relationship, like the patient–doctor relationship, is among the most professional types of interaction that can take place. It involves far more trust than traditional customer–sales representative relationships. To be a client, a customer must have confidence that he can place

Figure 4. Psychological input audit.

Psychological inputs I must obtain in order to prescribe a system for
_____ to improve the profit contri-
(Customer Account Name)
bution of its _____
(Customer Process or Function)

Other-than-profit values and considerations that must be acknowledged	Ingoing negative attitudes or adversary relationships that must be overcome
_____	_____
_____	_____
_____	_____
_____	_____
_____	_____
_____	_____
_____	_____
_____	_____

proprietary process knowledge in a seller's hands. A client relationship also involves a higher order of benefit than a sales representative can deliver. Satisfactory product performance, which is generally a sales representative's objective, is a minor benefit compared with the vital benefit of profit improvement, which the systems seller must deliver.

In addition to increased trust and a higher order of benefit, a client relationship also differs from a sales relationship in a third way. The relationship is non-adversary in nature. A seller positioned as a consultant does not compete against the client; they cooperate to help achieve client objectives. Instead of working in a win-lose situation, the consultant conducts a win-win relationship with every client. A second type of non-competitiveness occurs in the uniqueness of the seller's role. A customer can deal with many sales representatives. But a client can deal with only one consultant for each vital process. A systems seller can therefore be insulated from competition by adequately fulfilling the consultant role.

The increased professionalization that characterizes a client–consultant relationship occurs when the systems seller is able to meet three conditions:

1. Set mutually rewarding objectives that meet customer needs.
2. Establish a progressive schedule of planning and application sessions with the customer to achieve mutual objectives.
3. Construct a control procedure to ensure that every system is producing promised benefits on schedule.

Setting mutually rewarding objectives. To become skilled in setting mutually rewarding objectives, the systems seller must continually seek out the needs that underlie customer objectives. Needs are generally created by the awareness of a problem. Since the systems seller must function as a problem solver, the needs that generate the problems must be uncovered; these needs, in turn, provide the basis for customer objectives.

Establishing planning and application schedules. A systems seller is performing professionally if the question "When?" is never asked by customers. The answer must always be ready before the question can be asked. This comes about by imposing a time frame on the planning and application of each system. Scheduling objectives will be a resolution of two sets of needs: the seller's own need for enough time to do a thorough, professional job and the customer's need to begin deriving benefits from the system.

Constructing controls. The systems seller's planning and application schedules run the risk of becoming fictional unless they can be controlled against straying off target dates or failing to produce their promised benefits. The natural appendage to every schedule must therefore be a set of control procedures. These procedures take several forms: a simple probe into progress on an on-plan/off-plan basis, with no report required if the plan's schedule is being satisfactorily met; a written progress report; and a periodic progress meeting.

From a customer's point of view, controls provide the confidence to make a client relationship with a systems seller appear safe. Without controls, a client reverts to being a customer. Controls enable a customer to develop a sense of security that needs will be met without undue risk of catastrophic failure. They are, therefore, the foundation of the customer's comfort in believing that it is safe to be a client of the seller.

A control procedure for a consultant relationship requires a *monitor schedule* while a system is being installed, while it is operating, and as it is being added to. The objectives of the monitor schedule are twofold. First, a schedule allows seller and customer to keep their fingers on the pulse of what is happening in "real time" while it is actually happening. This enables them to share a common fact base, which is one of the most important things they can have in common. Second, a monitor schedule allows seller and customer to head off problems before the problems become bigger than both of them. By providing proper early warning, they can avoid surprises and plan together how to deal with critical issues. This is another one of the most important things a seller and customer can share. Solving common problems together is the main business of every consultant relationship.

A control procedure to monitor the progress of the relationship will generally be composed of three elements:

1. An *information-gathering* element that not only tells what is happening but also is sensitive enough to measure it.
2. A *review* element that provides periodic short-term reporting sessions, usually no less frequently than monthly, at which the system's operation can be "managed by exception." Under this approach, only exceptional deviations from plan are brought to attention for discussion and solution.
3. A *contingency* element that provides alternate remedies, planned in advance and held in ready reserve, that can be plugged into the system's operations on an on-line basis to remedy problems.

Converting Customers into Clients

A consultant cannot consult with a customer. A consultant requires a client. Customers and clients are very different people. Converting customers into clients is a major task for the systems seller.

If a seller allows a systems customer to remain a customer, the seller will be put at a serious disadvantage. The customer will treat the seller as an alternate supplier. As such, the customer will create a frankly competitive position with other suppliers. The seller will be forced to persuade the customer that the seller's system delivers the best benefits. Prominent among these benefits will probably have to be the "best price" from the customer's point of view.

The chief distinguishing characteristic of a client is a value-to-price orientation that favors value. A customer, on the other hand, is generally oriented toward price. The trade-off a client makes with a consultant about accepting a high price in return for added value can be expressed something like this:

"I will accept your high price as proof of your added value. But in return for the extra cost that I will incur, I want extra service. I will insist, therefore, that you recognize and respond to certain demands, which I will feel free to make on you and which I will consider to be my 'rights of clienthood.' "

The most generally accepted method of converting a customer into a client is to endow the customer with the rights of clienthood. A systems seller who wants to achieve a consultant's position may have to award as many as 15 rights to customers:

1. *"Cure Me"*
   Get things done—respond to my needs.
   Produce results fast because I have more needs.
2. *"Talk My Language"*
   Speak to me in profit-improvement language.
   Show me you identify with me and that you know my business.

3. *"Don't Surprise Me"*
   Install a control system so I can be comfortable.
   Let me share in evaluating our work together.
4. *"Level with Me"*
   Tell it like it is.
   Criticize constructively.
   Tell me what's wrong, but let me know what's right, too.
5. *"Get into My Business"*
   Become a part of my team.
   Be around—ask questions.
   Don't be disruptive.
6. *"Be Reasonable"*
   Give a superior value in relation to your superior price—
   superior service makes a high price reasonable.
7. *"Be Competent"*
   Give me the best you have.
   Be a real professional.
8. *"Teach Me"*
   While you sell or perform, teach me how.
   Share some of your experience and expertise with me and
   my people.
9. *"Take Leadership"*
   Get out in front of my problems.
   Roll up your sleeves and get your hands dirty in my operations.
10. *"Worry for Me"*
    Think hard about my problems.
    Let me know what you think even without my asking.
    Give me immediate access to you when I am worried—be
    available.
    Put my needs first—never mind anyone else.
11. *"Innovate"*
    Give me something that's better than you give anyone else.
    Make me proud—make me stand out.
    Apply yourself in a way that transcends normal bound-
    aries.
    Offer me options.
12. *"Be Faithful"*
    Keep our business confidential.
    Make your relationship with me personal and
    continuous—don't pass me along to others.

13. *"Be Motivated"*
    Show a strong desire to achieve our objectives.
    Be really interested in my problems.
    Don't leave a single stone unturned in looking for solutions.
14. *"Be Flexible"*
    Compromise with me once in a while but don't give in on what you know is vital.
15. *"Treat Me Like a Person, Not Just a Client"*
    Treat me like an equal—deal with me one-to-one.
    Don't talk down to me.
    Throw in a few "little extras" every now and then.
    Advise me on closely related matters even if you're not being paid for them.

What the rights of clienthood amount to is an expression of a customer's concern for the investment in a system, of the need for visibility of commitment, and of the dependency that must be placed on the seller's expertise. The seller must be sensitive to the customers' needs to receive their rights and to know that the seller will diligently adhere to them. Along with the profit-improvement benefits of the seller's system, recognition of customer rights of clienthood is the most important contributor to systems-selling success.

4

Product Desensitization

The most difficult aspect of positioning for systems selling is to stop selling products and equipment and to start selling the added financial values that a system can contribute to a customer's business. This requires more than merely substituting one vocabulary for another. It makes the seller substitute one manner of thinking for another. Before this can be done, however, the seller must first undergo a desensitization to traditional product affiliations.

Most sales representatives arrive at the proper systems-selling positioning by means of a two-stage process. The first stage is to forsake feature orientation for benefit orientation. This is the classic features-versus-benefits metamorphosis that many sellers are encouraged to undertake long before they come face to face with systems selling. But in systems selling, product benefits are insufficient reasons for a customer to buy.

Product benefits and equipment benefits attempt to describe what a product *is* in operating terms. Systems selling requires a seller to describe what a system *does* in financial terms. It is the end accomplishment of a system's benefits that must be sold.

Desensitizing a selling style from preoccupation with physical product features or their operating benefits is difficult because such a style is comfortable. It demands just a single-step translation: Here is a construction feature and here is its operating benefit (such as durability, flexibility, reliability, convertibility) one of the "abilities" that a particular material or a design technique can confer on a product. But customers cannot profit from abilities. They can only profit from the financial values that an ability can provide.

The second stage in translating features to benefits is the calculation of their dollarized benefit values. These values, referred to as incremental or added values, are the systems seller's stock in trade. In the systems-selling strategy, *a system's incremental values are the system*.

THE TRANSLATED DIALOG OF VALUE SELLING

Product desensitization starts with awareness that systems selling is a translated dialog. All systems components, including the systems seller, must be translated into a customer value. Hanging out a laundry list of components is meaningless unless their individual contribution to incremental value is quantified. Mentioning product, elaborating on the technological superiority of equipment, extolling its construction characteristics or other qualities are equally meaningless unless the incremental values of their existence in the system are quantified.

Translating product into benefit and then translating benefit into incremental value is a cast of mind. It is a consultative cast of mind because this is the way consultants must think. "What is the end result?" is their key question. They sensitize themselves to this sort of bottom-line thinking because they have learned that intermediate-line thinking fails to accomplish two objectives. It fails to position their customers as clients, since a client is a bottom-line beneficiary. And it fails to position themselves as consultants, since a consultant is a supplier of bottom-line benefits.

Nothing will deposition a systems seller faster or more certainly from a consultative stance than the seller's lapse back into product concentration. It is the systems seller's deadliest sin and an ever present pitfall. The words "the product" rather than "the value" lie poised from long habit on the tip of most sellers' tongues, ready to undo them. The best way to avoid falling into the pit is to learn to use the new frame of reference in parallel with the old one and translate-as-you-go. Whenever a product or any piece of hardware is mentioned or described, a good practice is to define it immediately in terms of its contribution to customer value. This is what customers do. Experienced systems customers have trained themselves to listen for the numbers. Systems sellers must become sensitive to this need and deliver the benefit that customers seek: quantification, not product.

5

Problem Solving

The ability to seek out and solve customer problems is the most important distinguishing characteristic of a good systems seller. The acid test of this fact can be demonstrated in this way: The hardware and software components of a seller's system may enjoy no superiority. In fact, they may be only equal to competition. They may actually be inferior. Furthermore, the seller's pricing policy may not be competitive. But as long as the seller's problem-solving capability is superior, success can occur.

From a customer's point of view, a "better system" is primarily differentiated on the basis of its seller's "better" problem-solving capability. This is validated by the system's superior ability to improve customer profit.

In Figure 5, the systems seller's consultant positioning is shown as a significant aid in penetrating the process by which customers make decisions so that sales can be won before the launching of competitive bids.

In the figure, a system sale starts with customer awareness that there is a problem in a major process. Its costs are too high or its efficiency is too low, either in an absolute sense or relative to comparable operations. Sometimes this awareness is generated by internal problems. At other times it may come from external triggers, such as a competitor's adoption of a

Figure 5. Systems seller's problem-solving positioning in customer decision-making process.

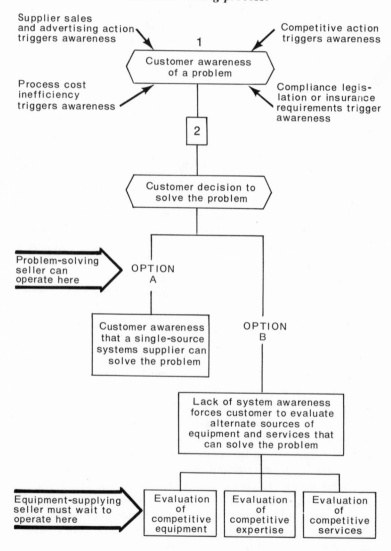

new solution, compliance legislation or insurance requirements that make new solutions mandatory, or a systems seller's promotional activity. It is the rule rather than the exception that such an external trigger will finally force a long-
suppressed internal awareness out into the open so that a customer must deal with it.

Once the problem has been identified, a decision can be
made to solve it. There are always two options. If Option A is
taken, the customer will act on the awareness that there is a
superior single-source supplier who can solve the problem by
means of a system. If the systems seller has properly assumed
a problem-solving position, the customer can often be influenced to take this step. This is the ideal point for the systems
seller to enter into the customer's decision-making process. A
consultant position gives the seller a license to step in and
operate at this level. If the seller can believably promise to
solve the customer's problem at this point, the sale may be
made without prolonged or repeated presentations or competitive price considerations. In this way, the seller can hold down
selling costs as well as serve the customer best by compressing
the time spent searching for a solution and the considerable
costs that can go with it.

If Option B is taken, however, the seller has lost the advantage. The customer's lack of awareness of a superior
single-source supplier forces an evaluation of alternate sources
of equipment, services, and expertise on an individual basis.

The systems seller may never be able to get back into the
ballgame once Option B has been taken. At best, it will probably not be under the advantageous conditions of Option A. The
contribution to a system's price of each and every component
will likely have to be laid bare to the customer. This can make
the system's price appear high. It can encourage prolonged
price debate and focus customer attention away from the system's end benefit of improved profit. A wide variety of solutions, some only partial and many of them unprofitable, will
also be suggested to the customer by competitors. These
suggestions can add to customer confusion and stretch out the
decision-making process or even postpone it indefinitely.

Solving Problems That Are Profitable to Solve

The ever present danger for the systems seller positioned as a consultative problem solver is to attempt the solution of any and all customer problems. Not all customer problems are profitable to solve. Only problems that can return a high profit contribution are worth solving. To be successful, the seller must accept the discipline to concentrate solely on problems whose solutions can yield superior profit.

The seller's best rule of thumb is to *solve problems that are worth solving with customers worth solving them for.*

This means that every systems seller will have a concentrated practice. It will be concentrated on solving a relatively small number of problems by means of a relatively small number of systems that are sold to a relatively small number of customers.

The relatively small number of problems that the systems seller will find most profitable to solve will be a minimal percentage of all the problems that, technically speaking, can be solved. In this sense, a systems seller's technical competence to solve customer problems will always exceed the profit-making justification for doing so. Because the desire to apply technical competence tends to outrun the financial return that can be obtained from it, the seller must avoid trying to find solutions to problems just because "we have the capability." This is the fallacy of *We did it because we could.* The seller must also avoid seeking out and serving customers just because "they have a problem." This is the fallacy of *We did it because they needed it.*

Adopting a Step-by-Step Problem-Solving Process

The systems seller's consultative problem-solving process is a five-step sequence of gaining successive agreements. It is based on the assumption that the solution to every problem can be found inside the problem itself and is susceptible to the systems seller's expertise. The problem-solving process brings both the seller and the problem together from the very beginning of the problem-solving approach, so that the seller works with the customer on a shared basis as they go along. This is why there should be no surprises at the end solution. By then, the customer's evolving expectations about the solution will have been validated.

Step 1: Agree on the problem. The first step in the consultative problem-solving process is for seller and customer to agree on exactly what the customer's problem is. To reach agreement, the seller will have to play two roles. One is the role of *auditor,* which requires interested attentiveness to the customer's history of the problem. The second role is that of *diagnostician,* which requires distinguishing the symptoms of the customer's problem from their probable causes.

Customer problems are typically expressed as symptoms. The first application of the systems seller's problem-solving expertise is to get behind the symptoms and treat the causes of high cost of processing, low effectiveness, or any other depressed profit situation. By backtracking on symptoms in order to reach their causes, the seller can define the true problem. The greatest danger is to mistake a symptom for a cause and to design a system around its solution.

When the systems seller and the customer have agreed on the nature of the customer's problem, both should fill in and sign a *statement of agreement on the problem,* shown in Figure 6.

Step 2: Agree on the objective of the solution. Once the problem has been agreed on, the second step is to reach agreement on the objective of the solution. By doing so, both the systems seller and the customer will have a clear mutual target for their work together. This step also avoids the famous last words of many systems customers, "But I didn't think *this* is what we'd come out with."

The ultimate objective of every solution to a systems problem is to help improve the profit contribution of a customer's process. The way to reach that goal may be to achieve new revenues. Or it may be to reduce present costs. These are not ultimate objectives since they contribute to profit improvement

Figure 6. Statement of agreement on the problem.

Customer Account Name _____

Division or Department _____

We agree that the problem(s) to be solved is/are_____

_____
(Nature of Problem[s])

which is/are found in the_____
(Customer Process or Function)

_____
(SIGNED) For the Customer

_____
(SIGNED) For the Seller

but do not represent improved profits in themselves. For this reason, they should be thought of as subobjectives.

Two other subobjectives often lead to new revenues and cost reduction. These objectives are improved quality of products and higher volume output. A higher level of product quality can come from improving the system's process. So can faster, higher-volume production. Neither of these objectives is an ultimate objective since each can contribute to profit improvement but does not represent improved profit in itself.

When the systems seller and the customer have agreed on the nature of their ultimate objectives, both should fill in and sign a *statement of agreement on the objectives to be achieved,* shown in Figure 7.

Step 3: Agree on the options. The third step is for the seller and the customer to agree on the options that are avail-

Figure 7. Statement of agreement on the objectives to be achieved.

Customer Account Name _____

Division or Department _____

We agree that the objective(s) to be achieved in solving the

problem(s) of _____
                         (Nature of Problem[s])

which is/are found in the_____
                              (Customer Process or Function)

is/are:

1. An improved contribution to profit of approximately

    $ __ , ___ , ___ or____ %

2. To be achieved by:

    Cost reduction of $ __ , ___ , ___

    New sales revenues of $__ , ___ , ___

    Both

    _____
                (SIGNED) For the Customer

    _____
                (SIGNED) For the Seller

able to achieve the objectives. The seller's prescriptions for systems should be the vehicles for implementing these options. Sometimes there will appear to be only one system that can solve the problem in the most cost-effective manner. In such a case, there will be only one option.

At other times, a range of systems can be proposed. Some will be more elaborate than others, with the promise of a higher or more certain achievement of the solution's objectives. Others may utilize leading-edge technology that carries exciting promises of achievement but at greater risk and cost. Additional options may include choices of financing and other services that can add or subtract costs or contribute additionally to profits.

When the systems seller and the customer have agreed on the options available to achieve the objectives, the seller has completed the preliminary teaching-learning exchange with the customer. The customer has taught the seller the nature of the problem. The seller has taught the customer what options are open to solve the problem.

Step 4: Agree on the seller's prescribed option. The fourth step is for the seller to narrow the options down to a single system and to obtain the customer's agreement that this system achieves the solution's objectives in the most cost-effective manner.

It is important that the seller press for agreement on *the system's achievement of the solution's objectives* and not on the system itself. This is because the customer must be regarded as the final authority on objectives. The seller must defer to the customer in this respect. Therefore, the seller must obtain initial agreement on anything that can affect customer objectives.

On the other hand, the seller must be regarded as the final authority on the components and performance of a system. The seller must earn the customer's respect for this expertise. To help accomplish a consultative position, the systems seller will have to call into use not just personal expertise but also company information and other support services as well as documentation from case history examples on the performance of similar problem-solving systems. The main purpose in rallying this backing for the seller's prescription is to rule out as much as possible debate on the merits of the prescribed system and to concentrate attention on the system's ability to achieve customer objectives.

Step 5: Agree on terms. The fifth and final step is for the seller and the customer to reach agreement on the terms under which the customer can obtain the beneficial objectives of the system. These are primarily concerned with price and its accompanying financing and leasing options. The seller must not

present these raw but in the context of their contribution to the
ultimate solution to the customer's problem—profit improvement.

The systems seller has two objectives in managing this
five-step problem-solving process. The system must be accepted. But over and above this objective, the seller's second
objective is to gain acceptance as an influencer inside the customer's company. This is the seller's optimal positioning.
When it is achieved, the seller is no longer an outside supplier.
Instead, the systems seller becomes an insider who can influence customer operations for mutual profit improvement.

6

Profit-Improvement Measurement

Systems customers define a problem as a cost that can be reduced or a sales opportunity that remains unfulfilled. Customers define a solution to a problem as a cost that has been reduced or sales revenue that has been gained. In either case, customer profit has been improved. The best rule of thumb for every systems seller to follow is that a customer problem has been solved only when the prescribed profit improvement has been produced by the seller's system.

Customers measure their solutions according to *incremental analysis*. This is sometimes called microanalysis, since it evaluates the new profit earned by a specific project such as a system.

There are three methods of incremental analysis that are commonly used to measure a system's problem-solving contribution: payback, discounted cash flow (DCF), and accounting rate of return (AROR).

Payback

The payback method measures problem solving according to how long it will take to recoup the cash outlay required to obtain a system. Payback is essentially a criterion of "cash at risk." If payback can be achieved quickly, the risk factor will be seen as low and the return will be high. If a system's benefits continue after payback, the return will be even higher.

Discounted Cash Flow

The DCF method measures problem solving by converting the cash values of a system's costs and benefits into a present-time value. Discounted cash flow analysis is usually used in conjunction with payback analysis and the AROR approach on major systems. There are two variations of the DCF method:

1. *Net present value* (*NPV*) applies a predetermined interest rate to discount future cash flow in order to match it with a system's required cash outlay. The interest rate may be based on a customer's cost of capital or an arbitrary "hurdle rate" that has been set as the minimum payback for new investments. A high net present value is a customer signal to proceed.

2. *Internal rate of return* (*IRR*) is similar to net present value but does not contain a predetermined discount factor. The IRR is the interest rate that discounts a system's net cash flow to zero present value when compared with its required cash outlay. If the IRR rate exceeds the hurdle rate, a customer will usually proceed.

Accounting Rate of Return

The AROR method measures problem solving by comparing the average income or expenses saved over the life of a system with the investment outlay required to obtain the system. The percentage rate of return that results is based solely on the incremental income generated by the system and reflects the earnings rate of return on the incremental investment. Many customers favor this method because it is oriented to their balance sheets and income statements even though it ignores the time value of money.

All three measurement methods have certain elements in common. They all use a basic costs-benefits analytical approach. All of them seek to determine the present value of a system investment on a cash basis, including the opportunity costs involved; the operating revenue; the operating costs; and the difference between operating revenue and operating costs, which equals the benefits.

Of the three methods, however, only the accounting rate of return relates to the return on investment, or ROI, which is used to evaluate total customer company performance. This total return on investment must be narrowed down to AROR in order to evaluate an incremental investment such as a specific system. A system's AROR can, therefore, be considered as the added rate of profit that the system can add to the customer company ROI.

The following example will show how the AROR method can help determine whether to lease or buy a system.

1. *AROR on short-term lease, with no investment shown on the balance sheet.*

System A is leased for $12,000 per year on a three-year lease. Projected labor-expense savings are $18,000 per year. The net benefits from expense savings are $6,000 per year.

$$\text{AROR} = \frac{\text{net income}}{\text{investment}} = \frac{\$6,000}{0} = \text{infinity}$$

2. *AROR on purchase, with investment shown on the balance sheet.*

System B is purchased for $60,000. Projected average expense savings are $6,000 per year for x years.

$$\text{AROR} = \frac{\text{average net income}}{\text{investment}} = \frac{\$6,000}{\$60,000} = 10\%$$

On a straight AROR basis, the lease alternative is more attractive than purchase. If discounted cash flow is used, the purchase decision improves in attractiveness because it takes into consideration the time value of money, which the accounting rate of return omits. This is a frequent dilemma. The optimal investment decision from a financial point of view may not be optimal from the point of view of the balance sheet and the total ROI that a customer company reports to its stockholders.

AROR/ROI Interrelationships

The interrelationship between ROI and AROR can be seen by noting the similarity between their formulas:

$$\text{ROI} = \frac{\text{net profit}}{\text{sales}} \times \frac{\text{sales}}{\text{investment}}$$

$$\text{AROR} = \frac{\text{net profit}}{\text{investment}}$$

For the application of the accounting rate of return, sales are eliminated from the ROI formula. This is because total customer company analysis is not relevant for most systems investments. The impact of most systems, even huge capital-intensive systems, becomes swallowed up in a customer's total ROI. The seller cannot identify an individual system's contribution when it is dispersed over such a broad base. Therefore, to make a system's incremental contribution measurable, its impact should be calculated according to AROR.

Net income is not the sole basis for determining AROR. Gross profit may be an appropriate measure of a system's income if no incremental operating costs are involved or if operating costs will be joint and cannot be separated on incremental sales. Contribution margin may also be an appropriate measure of system income if no incremental fixed costs are incurred or if fixed costs will be joint and cannot be separated.

How Customers Quantify Costs and Benefits

Customers speak a language of numbers when they attempt to quantify the added value of a system to their operations. The seller must become fluent in the same language. Some of the more familiar guidelines to "systems talk" are the following buzz words:

incremental investment—all outlays incident to placing a system into use, minus after-tax cash savings resulting from disposal of replaced equipment, minus costs avoided to maintain present equipment, and minus investment-tax credit if applicable.

revenue—income from a system's "plus sales."

benefits—the difference in net income between the present or competitive system and the proposed system, projected over the life of the system and averaged to an annual contribution.

7

Penetration

The art of penetrating a customer account requires agility in dealing with four basic organization structures that exist in every business: the *power structure*, which has both apparent and hidden sources; the *group structure*, which has formal and informal relationships that interact, and often counteract each other; the *role structure*, with its imposed and self-perceived performance requirements; and the *status structure*, which confers rank on customer decision makers and influencers.

Customer organization structures, like the human beings who compose them, are living organisms. They have a life of their own. They have an individual life-style, codes of behavior, standards of performance, and criteria for admission—especially for outside influencers such as systems sellers. In order to qualify for admission, a systems seller must become knowledgeable about a customer's organization structures and their leaders, so that he or she will be perceived by them *as a compatible adder of value to their power, performance, and status.*

Penetrating with Negotiation

Negotiation is the systems seller's main penetration tool. It is the act of mutual bargaining over optional ways of achieving a common objective, so that when the objective is reached both negotiators win. The customer wins the profit-improvement benefits from a system. The seller wins the profit-improvement benefits from selling or leasing it.

Negotiation is a reciprocal process. Both parties must openly and honestly develop the customer's needs. Then both parties must discuss the best way the customer's needs can be fulfilled while at the same time making sure that the seller's needs are also fulfilled. Because seller and customer develop the customer's needs together, the climate of a negotiated sale is we-oriented from the beginning. It says to the customer that *we* are both concerned with serving *your* needs.

When the customer's needs are revealed to both the customer and the seller, and when it can be shown that those needs are served best by the seller's system, both of them know that their individual self-interests will be met by the negotiation. At this point, the customer can take the first step toward feeling comfortable in the relationship.

To penetrate a customer organization by negotiation, a systems seller must understand three aspects of the negotiation process:

1. Negotiation requires a win-win orientation. Both seller and customer must win a significant new benefit.
2. Negotiation requires that both seller and customer perceive each other as equals. Each must hold equal respect for the other as an essential contributor to the fulfillment of both parties' common needs.
3. Negotiation requires that both seller and customer lay their needs on the table and that they then proceed to satisfy the customer's needs in the way that is best for both of them.

The give-and-take of the negotiation process by which the customer's needs are learned must be managed by the seller. It is the seller's job to take charge of the process. The best way the seller can conduct a negotiated sales process is by practicing the art of negotiative questioning with customers. There are six basic types of negotiating questions:

1. *Why* questions that ask the customer: "Why do you manage your operation the way you do?" "Why would you perceive new options as being valuable?"

2. *What* questions that ask the customer: "What do you think would happen if certain things were to be done in a different way?" "What happened when operations were innovated or renovated in the past?" "What could be done better than the way it is being done now?"

3. *How* questions that ask the customer: "How do you feel about current operations and their results?" "How might your operations be conducted in a more cost-efficient manner?" "How can innovations be best introduced?"

4. *Who* questions that ask the customer: "Who in the company could benefit most from change?" "Who might be hurt or inconvenienced?" "Who are the chief decision makers and their influencers?"

5. *When* questions that ask the customer: "When do you sense the best timing will be for a presentation so that it will have the greatest chance for acceptance?" "When do you plan to take action?"

6. *Where* questions that ask the customer: "Where can I gain access to the internal information I require to custom-tailor my presentation?" "Where can I validate the external information I have acquired?"

Principles of Penetrant Negotiation

The principles of penetrant negotiation are based on effective customer relations. Seven principles are the most important for a systems seller to practice:

1. Have respect for the customer. Earn his respect. Be yourself so he can know and respect the real "you." Avoid trying to dominate the relationship so that both of you can value it equally.

2. Act like a consultant. This means substitute a teaching role for sales aggressiveness. The first thing to teach the customer is how to become a client. This means penetrating his traditional customer defensiveness with a partnership approach that makes each system sale a true joint venture.

3. Be open, intellectually accessible, and authentic. Disclose yourself and your motives to your customer. Start out by

frankly and unashamedly admitting your self-interest in every transaction. Lay it on the line. In turn, allow the customer to reciprocate.

4. Before anything else, set mutually agreeable objectives. Once the end objectives are accepted, the strategic means can be worked out. Spell out clearly how achievement of the objectives will benefit each of you.

5. Be emphatic about the customer's needs. Sense problem situations from a customer perspective. Play back your understanding so the customer can validate your assumptions. Validation is the first step toward the successive agreements that must occur in negotiation.

6. Communicate in a way that advances the relationship by adding new insights and revelations, and by reinforcing feedback. Discuss rather than debate.

7. Acknowledge customer needs for defense mechanisms. Don't try to beat your way through them or tear them down. Create a relationship that will make customary defenses unnecessary.

How to Negotiate with Power Sources

The ability to make system decisions is solely within a customer's power. The systems seller has no comparable power. The seller's only leverage against a customer's power is a system's ability to improve customer profit. This ability allows the seller to influence a customer's decision. It must be fully used. This means two things. The seller must know everything that is knowable about how a profit-improving system can be designed to meet customer needs. The seller must also know everything that is knowable about the customer's power structure.

Power is the ability to make, prevent, or influence a decision. Very few decision makers have that much power. Instead, power is typically limited and fragmented. The systems seller must find out who has what type of power. Only then can a cost-effective selling strategy be planned. It will be helpful for the seller to seek out the location of three power sources:

1. The power to say yes. A yes-sayer is the seller's prime target. If the seller can identify a yes-sayer's needs and influence them directly on a one-to-one basis, the maximum opportunity will exist for selling a system.

2. The power to say no. A no-sayer is the salesman's prime potential adversary. A no-sayer does not generally have the power to say yes. But a no-sayer may have the power to kill a system proposal before it can come to the attention of a yes-sayer. To sell successfully, the seller will have to neutralize no-sayers or convert them into allies.

3. The power to influence the yes-sayers and the no-sayers. An influencer has only implicit power. But it can often swing the balance of decision making in the seller's favor. Influencers can be especially important in helping override highly detailed questions of system price or performance. The seller's task is to mobilize an influencer's influence in a way that helps the seller sell a system.

How to Deal with Yes-Sayers

Yes-sayers have official power. Theirs is the power of position. It is usually symbolized by a title that expresses the power to compel compliance.

Yes-sayers must be dealt with along the lines of their needs to act in conformity to two roles they play simultaneously. One role is their self-perceived status as decision makers. The other role is imposed on them by their titular position. If a seller brings these two roles into conflict with each other, the yes-sayer will probably say no or say nothing.

Fortunately, both roles of the yes-sayer converge around a major common need: the need to improve the profitability of the organization. Appeals to yes-sayers should therefore be based on the projected improvements in profit that the seller's system can contribute to the yes-sayer's operations.

There are two other important appeals to which yes-sayers are usually responsive. The first is an appeal to maintain the organization's image of efficiency, modernity, and quality performance in the minds of its customers, competitors, employees, investors, and others who compose its constituents. The second is an appeal to the yes-sayer's personal value system, which has a high probability of assigning good grades to the concepts of managing a significant process improvement, presiding over a respected and well-reputed operation, and taking prudent risks.

Here is a checklist of appeals to yes-sayers:

1. Profit improvement and increased cost efficiency.
2. Improved organizational image in terms of operational efficiency, modern methods, leading-edge technology, and quality of both performance and product.
3. Compatibility of a system's benefits with personal values such as being respected and well reputed, being on top of things, managing in a progressive fashion, and being a wise evaluator of risk.

How to Deal with No-Sayers

No-sayers often have official power. They may be second in command and report to a yes-sayer or they may have a political power base unheralded by a high title. Sometimes they are deliberately encouraged by a yes-sayer to perform a control function by acting as devil's advocates.

No-sayers perceive their roles as saying no. Even when they are unable to find any reason to say no, they often tend to use their favorite word anyway in giving tacit agreement: "I can find *no* reason not to go ahead." The seller must communicate with no-sayers in their own terms. They must be deprived of any reason to say no to installing a system and still be allowed to fully exercise their negative screening approach.

This means that the seller will have to rule out with a no-sayer on a point-by-point basis why there is no reason that the seller's system should not be employed. This may require infinitely refined selling. The no-sayer may be interested in the system's contribution to improved profit. But an even greater interest may be directed to the bells, whistles, and flags of its composition, to the contribution to cost and efficiency of each component, and to its competitive assets or liabilities. Risk taking must be minimized in keeping with a no-sayer's value system that emphasizes caution, conformity, cost reduction, a tight control system, and the development of a high level of confidence before finding no reason not to go ahead. To meet these needs, the seller may have to engage in exhaustively detailed presentations of a system's credentials. Here is a checklist of appeals to no-sayers:

1. Cautious decision making based on fair and full evaluation of measurable facts and figures.
2. Conformity to either what is or what is rapidly becoming standard industry practice as a part of sound, conservative operating policy.
3. Demonstrable cost reduction accomplished by inauguration of new efficiencies or elimination of old inefficiencies.
4. A tight control system to measure operational cost efficiency and to apply immediate remedial action wherever indicated.
5. Confidence acquired from independent evaluation of claims, customer testimonials, and personal visits to similar installations.

How to Deal with Influencers

Influencers may have either official or political pull, which they apply to decision makers, often swaying them. Influencers are the most difficult power wielders to identify. Many of them are obscure. Since their power takes the form of personal influence, they do not necessarily hold high titles. In fact, many influencers are technical experts who function at middle organizational levels but whose knowledge is called on by yes-sayers as a vital factor in their decision making.

In addition to the power they are given because of their expertise, influencers may hold political power that a yes-sayer can use to feel out and manipulate the political reaction to decisions. Holders of social power in the organization or community may also be influential in recommending action to a yes-sayer.

Finding the hidden sources of influence in an organieation is a difficult assignment. Once identified, they must be dealt with individually on the basis of their relevant power. The influencer who holds expert power in technology, finance, or operations must be approached in technical terms with facts and figures from respected sources. The seller's technical support resources can help. So can case histories, customer testimonials, and demonstration visits by customers to similar system installations. Political and social power holders must also be influenced in terms of their own interests, which will be principally concerned with interpersonal relationships and personal values and how the seller's system will affect them. The seller will also be wise to emphasize how these benefits can be communicated in the most positive manner throughout the organization, so that the influencers' images will be enhanced in the eyes of superiors, peers, and the organizational community at large. No important organizational toes can be stepped on. No empires can be invaded or eliminated, nor can entrenched power wielders be displaced. In short, the political and social structure, must be preserved. Here is a checklist of appeals to influencers:

Influencers with a technical power base
1. Offer facts and figures to bear out claims attested to by respected independent or third-party sources.
2. Present case history documentation.
3. Quote customers' technical testimonials.
4. Encourage personal visits to similar installations.

Influencers with a political and social power base
1. Emphasize beneficial effects on interpersonal relations of all people importantly affected, with specific reference to the absence of career threats and maintenance or enhancement of political and official position in the power structure.
2. Offer aid in communicating benefits smoothly and fluently throughout the organization and its community.

Organization Analysis

Organization analysis is an ongoing, never-ending task. It is always a challenge, and there are several reasons why it tends to remain so despite a seller's best efforts, and perhaps even best hopes, to consider the job finished once and for all:

1. Organizations are becoming more and more complex, which makes them harder to penetrate.
2. Managers shift rapidly from one job to another, removing them from their sponsorship role in functions where sellers have become dependent on their patronage.
3. While individual decision makers still authorize purchase decisions, the trend is for major decisions to be made by expert groups composed of different specialized disciplines.
4. Cost reduction and profit improvement are becoming key objectives in virtually all operating areas of most businesses, adding to the difficulties in needs analysis that sellers face.
5. An acquisition can change the seller's ballgame overnight.

There are three areas of knowledge a seller must continually renew in order to ensure the required penetrating capability to sell systems. One is the *individual power-holder patterns*. A second is the *organization interaction patterns* in a customer account. The third is the *organization characteristics* of the account.

INDIVIDUAL POWER-HOLDER PATTERNS

Individual decision makers make an organization go. *The* organization is really *their* organization. The systems seller must analyze a customer's power structure, role structure, and leadership patterns in order to know how to answer the central question "To *whom* must I penetrate?"

Figure 8 suggests useful criteria for analyzing a customer organization's leadership to learn more about systems decision makers.

ORGANIZATION INTERACTION PATTERNS

Every organization is an endless chain of interactions. At times they are smooth. At other times they seethe. The seller must keep on top of three major varieties of patterns: the

Figure 8. Criteria for analyzing a customer organization's leadership.

ORGANIZATION POWER STRUCTURE

Power holder's name _____

- ☐ Position power: Has authority or is strategically positioned.
- ☐ Power over: Controls key groups or resources.
- ☐ Power to decide and act.
- ☐ Power to prevent decisions and action.
- ☐ Expert power: Has valued expertise.
- ☐ Power to help.
- ☐ Power to hinder.
- ☐ Power to reward.
- ☐ Power to punish.
- ☐ Personal power: Has influence with key people.
- ☐ Power of respect: May not be liked but commands respect.
- ☐ Power to recommend: Does staff work for decision makers.

ORGANIZATION LEADERSHIP PATTERN

Leader's name _____

- ☐ Autocratic
- ☐ Custodial and maintenance
- ☐ Supportive and consultative
- ☐ Integrative and participative
- ☐ Directive and forceful
- ☐ Free reign and laissez faire
- ☐ Bureaucratic
- ☐ Collegial and team building
- ☐ Exploitive and dog-eat-dog
- ☐ Primarily task-oriented
- ☐ Primarily people-oriented
- ☐ Balance of task- and people-oriented

ROLE STRUCTURE

Role Player's Name _____

- ☐ Decision maker
- ☐ Decision recommender
- ☐ Decision implementer
- ☐ Help seeker
- ☐ Help provider
- ☐ Answer seeker
- ☐ Information source
- ☐ Constructive critic

(*continued*)

Figure 8 (continued).

- ☐ Problem definer
- ☐ Problem-solving partner
- ☐ Early-warning alerter
- ☐ Protective defender
- ☐ Opinion gatherer
- ☐ Cooperative follower
- ☐ Introducer to key people
- ☐ Adviser and counselor
- ☐ Smoother of troubled waters
- ☐ Innovative suggester
- ☐ Interference runner
- ☐ Guide in avoiding political and power pitfalls
- ☐ Sorter of causes from symptoms
- ☐ Astute evaluator of proposals
- ☐ Shrewd idea packager
- ☐ Strategy proposer
- ☐ Freedom giver (allows me to contact other key people)
- ☐ Active supporter
- ☐ Devil's advocate
- ☐ Emotional antagonist
- ☐ Exploitive manipulator
- ☐ Unreasonable demander
- ☐ Devious misleader

- ☐ Self-centered games player
- ☐ Machiavellian conniver
- ☐ Self-insistent aggressor
- ☐ Spineless temporizer
- ☐ Pleader for exceptions
- ☐ Domineering arm twister
- ☐ Oily politician
- ☐ Ineffectual glad-hander
- ☐ Truth twister
- ☐ Behind-the-back critic
- ☐ Petty faultfinder
- ☐ Shrewd delayer and procrastinator
- ☐ Put-down artist
- ☐ Unscrupulous negotiator
- ☐ Rumormonger
- ☐ Character assassin
- ☐ Grudge nurser
- ☐ Credit claimer and blame delegator
- ☐ Obstacle builder
- ☐ Unethical attacker
- ☐ Popularity seeker
- ☐ Self-pitying "weeper"
- ☐ Apathetic resenter
- ☐ Passed-over nonentity

---

type of leadership exerted by decision makers, the characteristics of the organization's one-to-one interactions, and the tone and texture of intergroup relations. Figure 9 suggests useful criteria for analyzing a customer organization's interaction patterns. Use the criteria as a checklist to raise the level of your consciousness about how things get done in a customer's buying process.

Figure 9. Criteria for analyzing a customer organization's interaction patterns.

KEY DECISION MAKER'S LEADERSHIP STYLE

Decision maker's name _____

- ☐ Taskmaster: Gets things done
- ☐ Stabilizer: Maintains harmony.
- ☐ Politician: Good navigator.
- ☐ Conceptualizer: Transmits ideas.

- ☐ Integrator: Helps people work together.
- ☐ Maverick: Wavemaker.
- ☐ Bureaucrat: Enforces corporate policy.
- ☐ Strategy maker: Sets policy.

CHARACTERISTIC INTERACTIONS AMONG GROUPS

Group leaders' names _____

- ☐ Team up to make their views prevail.
- ☐ Hostile to each other.
- ☐ Suspicious of each other.
- ☐ Have conflicting objectives.
- ☐ Exchange information freely.
- ☐ Exchange little or no information.
- ☐ Agree on most matters.
- ☐ Disagree on most matters.
- ☐ Respect each other.

- ☐ Vie with each other for power.
- ☐ Open to each other's influence.
- ☐ Resist and resent each other's influence.
- ☐ Like each other.
- ☐ Dislike each other.
- ☐ Accommodate each other.
- ☐ Rigid in dealing with each other.
- ☐ Frustrate each other.

CHARACTERISTIC INTERACTIONS AMONG DECISION MAKERS

Decision makers' names _____

- ☐ Think alike on most matters.
- ☐ Think differently on most matters.

- ☐ Support each other's views.
- ☐ Oppose each other's views.
- ☐ Like each other.

(continued)

Figure 9 (continued).

☐ Partners in a win-win
relationship.
☐ Compete in a win-lose
relationship.
☐ Dislike each other.
☐ Work well together.
☐ Frustrate each other.
☐ Emotionally compatible.
☐ Emotional antagonists.
☐ Secure in the power each has.
☐ Engaged in a power struggle.
☐ Tolerant of each other.
☐ Jealous of each other.
☐ Similar personalities.
☐ Conflicting personalities.

☐ Suspicious and try to
outmaneuver each other.
☐ Work well as a team.
☐ Ignore each other.
☐ Flexible in dealing with each
other.
☐ Resolve conflict in dealing
with each other.
☐ Stir up conflict in dealing with
each other.
☐ Open to each other's views.
☐ Resistant to each other's
views.
☐ Support each other.
☐ Undercut each other.

ORGANIZATION CHARACTERISTICS

Every organization is characterized by seven attributes that sellers must analyze in order to make penetration in the most cost-effective manner. These characteristics are:

1. Climate.
2. Self-image.
3. Personality.
4. Tempo.
5. Value orientation.
6. Political structure.
7. Decision-making criteria.

Figure 10 suggests useful criteria for analyzing a customer organization's characteristics. Use the criteria as a checklist to raise the level of your consciousness about key account attributes.

Whether a customer organization is open or closed, whether it is friendly or hostile, whether it is suspicious or

Figure 10. Criteria for analyzing a customer organization's characteristics.

Climate

- ☐ Politically exploitive
- ☐ Ritualistically bureaucratic
- ☐ Friendly, relaxed, and informal
- ☐ Paternalistic and protective
- ☐ Traditionbound and past-oriented
- ☐ Erratic, impulsive, and wheel-spinning
- ☐ Status quo and maintenance-oriented
- ☐ Warm and supportive
- ☐ No-nonsense and businesslike

Personality

- ☐ Conflicted and divisive
- ☐ Confused and unsure
- ☐ Hypersensitive and defensive
- ☐ Apathetic and listless
- ☐ Arrogant and superior
- ☐ Maturely self-assured
- ☐ Energetic and adaptive
- ☐ Nervous and under stress
- ☐ Rigid and inflexible

Decision-Making Criteria

- ☐ Vendor reputation
- ☐ Primarily price-oriented
- ☐ Perceived value based on cost-benefits analysis
- ☐ Quality
- ☐ Service
- ☐ Technical superiority
- ☐ Reliability

Self-Image

- ☐ "We're Number One."
- ☐ "We're Number Two but gaining."
- ☐ "We're the young comers."
- ☐ "We're the mavericks of the industry."
- ☐ "We're the statesmen of the industry."
- ☐ "We're the high-growth company."
- ☐ "We're not the biggest, but we are the best."

Political Structure

- ☐ Dirty politics abound and intrigue is a way of life.
- ☐ Political maneuvering is carried on more or less ethically.
- ☐ The strong intimidate the weak at every possible opportunity.
- ☐ Politics are largely defensive: "Protect your flank at all times."
- ☐ Self-serving alliances are opportunistically formed and dissolved.
- ☐ Power holders use every strategy to retain and augment their power.
- ☐ Little political behavior exists and does not hurt the organization.

(continued)

Figure 10 (continued).

Tempo	*Value Orientation*
☐ "We move quicker than our competition."	☐ Management by objective philosophy
☐ "We move planfully and deliberately."	☐ Task achievement and limited goal attainment
☐ "We are opportunistic and move in the direction of the best profit opportunities."	☐ Improvement and innovation
	☐ Technological superiority
	☐ Market and customer service
☐ "We are slow to move and we resist change."	☐ Risk-free survival
☐ "We tend to run in circles."	☐ Planned, unspectacular growth
☐ "We think for a long time and then move fast."	☐ Product orientation
	☐ Short-term profit
☐ "We tend to go off halfcocked and then correct our mistakes."	☐ Long-term profit
	☐ Market domination
	☐ Increasing market share
	☐ Maintenance of status quo
	☐ Balance between profit and service to the community

accepting, or acts paternalistically or as a partner is as much determined by how wisely and how well it is penetrated as by its own traditions, characteristics, and style. A systems seller approaches a customer organization as an outside influencer. As long as the seller remains outside, the seller's influence will be adulterated. Only if the seller becomes an inside influencer—penetrating a customer's organization structure to influence decision makers—can systems be successfully sold.

8

Partnering

The basic approach of penetrant negotiation is to make a customer an ally, not an adversary. The major area of alliance to seek out is mutual profit improvement. Two people whose relationship with each other is built around mutual profit improvement are business *partners*. Only partners can maximize the values of negotiation.

Common Denominators of Partnering

All partnering is based on four common denominators:

1. Partners have *common objectives*. Each partner wants to improve his or her pride and profit.
2. Partners have agreed on *common strategies* for achieving their objectives. Their methods are initially based on mutual need seeking and then on mutual need fulfillment. In both cases, needs are arrived at through negotiation.
3. Partners are at *common risk*. Each partner has something of equal value, or at least significant value, to gain or lose.
4. Partners have a *common defense* against all others who are not included in the partnership. Each party deals as

65

an equal. Outsiders range from being less equal to
being perceïved as competitors.

Cooperative negotiation strategies enable partners to treat
each other as equals. This is the principal rule of partnerships.
There are ten additional rules that can help in selecting and
applying cooperative negotiation strategies.

1. Add value to each other. Teach each other new ways
   to improve personal actualization and professional
   productivity so that both partners profit by the relationship.
2. Be supportive of each other, not competitive. Form a
   staunch team.
3. Avoid surprises. Plan your work together and work
   according to your plan.
4. Be open and aboveboard. Always level with each
   other.
5. Enter into each other's frame of reference. Learn
   each other's perceptions so that you can see things
   from the other's point of view. Learn each other's
   assumptions so that each of you can understand the
   other's expectations of the partnership.
6. Be reliable. Partners must be there for each other
   when they are needed.
7. Anticipate opportunities and capitalize on them.
   Forecast problems and steer the partnership around
   them. Keep the partnership out of trouble. If trouble
   is unavoidable, give the partnership a head start in
   solving it.
8. Do your homework. Know what's happening in the
   area of the partnership's operations so you can make a
   professional contribution to its activities.
9. Treat each other as people, not just as functionaries.
   Be willing to provide the personal "little extras" that
   make a partnership a humane as well as a mighty
   force.
10. Enjoy the relationship and make it enjoyable for your
    partner. Both of you should prefer to work within the

partnership rather than any other relationship because it is one of the most rewarding associations either of you has ever had.

In systems selling, the partners are sharing in improved profit. This is the partnership's prime benefit. The second major benefit that partners can confer on each other is the shared experience of learning together just how their profits can be improved. A partnership should be a breeding ground for generating new knowledge of profit making and putting it to work with shared faith and shared apprehension. The act of learning together is one of the strongest bonding agents in a partnership. It is the growth element in the relationship because it ensures that *both* partners will grow.

The third attribute of a successful partnership is mutual support. Each partner divides the relationship's labor according to individual capabilities. The complementary nature of the relationship enhances each of them. Conversely, each partner is diminished by the absence of the other.

Understanding a Partner's Motivations

The customer decision makers who must be partnered by a systems seller are multimotivated. They rarely act on the basis of one motive alone. Status, money, autonomy, and self-realization propel them. Of all their drives, three are likely to be major: power, achievement, and affiliation.

The power motive. Managers like to direct, influence, and control others; they like power. Power is measured by three standards: (1) access to or control over important resources; (2) ability to impose will on others; (3) the extent to which others and the flow of events can be influenced. Power can give its holder the right to act or to prevent others from acting. Power *over* people, or power *with* them, is called leadership. It may be as coercive as that of the Exploiter, as seductive as that of the Paternalistic Autocrat, as manipulative as that of the Machiavellian, or as constructive as that of the Integrator.

The seller must learn to cope with the power structure in

customer organizations. Power can be recognized by its two faces. One is *personalized*. The other is *socialized*. Personalized power is based on a dominance-submission relationship, a win-lose type of interaction. It is self-aggrandizing at the expense of others. Socialized power, on the other hand, is used for the benefit of others. It helps people feel confident and competent, so that they can achieve common objectives. It is energizing, sustaining, and supportive.

The achievement motive. Entrepreneurial managers are high achievers. They are task-oriented: They initiate action, they don't merely react. It is not money, power, or a need for the affection of their associates that primarily drives them. It is the urge to achieve for its own sake. Sellers who are also high achievers should find it mutually rewarding to negotiate with the entrepreneurial type of manager. Even if this is not the case, they can work well with Achievers by knowing what inpels them.

The affiliation motive. Both the power motive and the affiliation motive are geared to people. One involves dominance, the other is concerned with maintaining good interpersonal relations. The achievement motive is naturally task-oriented. Managers such as the Missionary have a drive to relate to people, to be liked and accepted by them, and to belong to desirable reference groups. Most effective managers rate high on affiliation, as do the best sellers. Affiliators expect a good deal of interaction. The most effective managers are relatively high achievers and affiliators. In contrast, ineffective managers are likely to be low achievers but excessively high affiliators.

Partnering a Customer's Decision Makers

Every decision maker can be considered as a fraction. The denominator is always the same: needs and aspirations that are common to us all. Every numerator, though, is exceptional. Numerators are composed of individual differences. In order to penetrate a customer organization, the systems seller must analyze what is individual as well as what is common. This can be done by answering two questions: Who are the decision makers I can partner with? Who are the decision makers I will have difficulty partnering with?

DECISION MAKERS WHO MAKE GOOD PARTNERS

There are eight types of decision makers who have high partnering potential. Figure 11 summarizes their principal characteristics and most probable negotiating modes.

The Bureaucrat. Despite negative connotations of the word, it is generally not difficult to partner a bureaucrat. The bureaucratic self-image is rational and systemized. Policies, procedures, and rules govern all actions. Although friendships and jealousies may abound among bureaucrats, and while politicking may be a favorite indoor sport, the selling climate is impersonal. By definition, there are several levels of management and a complex of functional areas in which things get done systematically but not speedily. Divergent personalities and individual eccentricities are discouraged. The organizational way of doing things must be followed to the letter.

Selling to a bureaucracy depends on understanding its traditional nature and cultivating its key decision makers. It is almost always a long-term process.

The Zealot. Zealots are organizational loners. Although intensely concerned for the organization's welfare, the Zealot has an apostolic zeal for pet projects, which are always presented as being precisely what the organization needs most. The Zealot is usually competent. Other people's ideas, however, go largely ignored. Individual and organizational sensitivities are routinely stepped on. A systems seller may find Zealots bothersome, overly demanding, and at times pests. Zealots negotiate by bludgeoning sellers, although they welcome with open arms anyone who can help in attaining their objectives. Two dangers are ever present. Zealots can be possessive. Since they tend to divide the world into "friends" and "enemies," the seller must be wary of becoming unduly identified with the Zealot and the Zealot's causes. Second, the

Figure 11. *High-partnering-potential decision makers.*

MANAGER TYPE	CHARACTERISTICS	NEGOTIATING MODES
Bureaucrat	Rational, formal, impersonal, politely proper, well disciplined, jealous of rights and prerogatives, well versed in the organization's "rocks and shoals."	Follows the letter of the law. Stickler for rules and procedures. Task-oriented, less concerned with people. Logical strategist but may be a nitpicker. Predictable negotiator.
Zealot	A competent loner, impatient, outspoken, overly independent, self-sufficient, jumps the traces, a nuisance to the Bureaucrats, insensitive to the feelings of others, minimal to modest political skills, fair but demanding.	Devoted to "the good of the organization." Excessively task-oriented but little concern for people. Aggressive and domineering strategist. Blunt, direct negotiator who may be self-seeking but supports allies fiercely.
Executive	Dominant but not domineering, directive but permits considerable freedom, consultative but not really participative, sizes up people well but relates to them on a surface level, cordial but keeps others at arm's length.	Concerned for the good of the organization. Wins respect. High task orientation. Polished and professional managerial style. Assertive but fair negotiator. Adroit strategist, flexible in switching from cooperative to defensive negotiation strategies.
Integrator	Egalitarian, supportive, participative, excellent interpersonal skills, superior insight, a team builder, catalyst, adept at unifying different values, subtle leader, prefers group decision making.	Shares leadership. Thinks in terms of associates rather than subordinates. Permits great freedom and authority. Welcomes the ideas of others. Open and honest negotiator. Collaborative strategist geared to win-win relationships.

Figure 11 (continued).

MANAGER TYPE	CHARACTERISTICS	NEGOTIATING MODES
Advocate	Normally competent, assertive and cooperative when not threatened, oriented to a functional area but not at the expense of the overall operation, politically skilled, not a loner but will not stick his neck out unless supported by the group.	Organizationally attuned. High task orientation. Good interpersonal skills. Strategies are cooperative if they benefit the Advocate and are for the good of the organization. Strategies are aggressive or defensive if self-interests are threatened. Excellent negotiator, pragmatic, realistic.
Developer	Trustful of people, intent on helping them actualize their potential, excellent human relations skills, wins personal loyalty, builds a supportive and achieving climate, fine coach and counselor.	Very high people orientation. Although productivity is superior, at times people considerations take precedence. Strategies are collaborative. Negotiations tend to be largely based on human considerations.
Gamesman	Fast-moving, flexible, upwardly mobile, impersonal, autonomous, risk-taking, assertive and intent on winning, innovative, takes no pleasure in another's loss or defeat, opportunistic but not unethical, not depressed by setbacks.	Wants to be respected as a winner who builds a winning team. Enjoys the game of winning within the organization's rules. Enjoys competition, jockeying, and maneuvering. Sharp, skilled, and tough negotiator. Win-win strategist.
Paternalistic Autocrat	Benevolent, patronizing, may be condescending and protective, rarely open to new ideas that are "not invented here," not consultative or participative.	Binds people emotionally. Makes them feel guilty if they disagree. Good people skills. Benevolent strategist if not crossed. Supportive negotiator for people who agree.

seller's patience may wear thin. Many judgments Zealots routinely make about sellers are based on zany personal criteria.

The Executive. Executive types have been called "polished autocrats." They are professional managers, battlewise, dominant, firm-minded, and strong-willed. They get the most out of people by accurately perceiving their strengths and limitations. Executives set a no-nonsense tempo and tone in their organizations. They are sensitive to people but do not get involved with them emotionally. Negotiating with an Executive type is a straightline matter of providing demonstrable benefits. An Executive looks to a seller for incremental values. If they cannot be perceived, negotiation will most likely end promptly.

The Integrator. Integrators are team-building managers. They are among the easiest to negotiate with. Integrators perceive their role not so much as decision makers as managing the decision-making process by consensus and collaboration. The Integrator is seen as a leader, catalyst, and constructive stimulant whose job is to create a climate that emphasizes superior task accomplishment, individual growth and success, mutual respect and cooperation. Since most of the Integrator's decisions are group decisions, the seller must not only partner with Integrators but also with key team members.

The Advocate. Advocates are interested in the good of their overall organizations but much more concerned for the interests of their particular division, department, or function. Their perspective is more limited than that of the Executive. Advocates are usually fair and supportive. They cooperate readily with sellers but can become defensive if sellers attempt to move in aggressively. Anything that promises to help an Advocate's part of the organization will encourage cooperative strategy making.

The Developer. Developers define their roles primarily in terms of actualizing people, maximizing motivation and satisfaction, and producing superior levels of achievement. People are of prime importance to a Developer. Negotiating with Developers is generally pleasant. It does, however, require a high degree of interpersonal skills.

The Gamesman. Gamesmen run on fast tracks. Highly

analytical, flexible, fast moving, competitive, sharp, and aggressive, they love playing the game of success. They are adept in-fighters but win respect while doing so. Their preoccupation is with forming and reforming winning teams. The seller must become a team member. Like the Executive, the Gamesman relates well without becoming involved in emotional entanglements. Wisely risk taking, innovative, and strategically keen, Gamesmen enjoy jockeying and maneuvering. Since a Gamesman respects only people who are shrewd and adroit, this type of manager will challenge every negotiation skill that a seller possesses. Yet Gamesmen negotiate within the rules and will be unusually cooperative if they believe they can win.

The Paternalistic Autocrat. Autocrats see their role as all-knowing, somewhat patronizing authority figures who demand personal loyalty from subordinates. Friction and conflict are smoothed over. Autocrats can be very kind and considerate but these traits are likely to vanish instantly if a seller promotes ideas that are antagonistic to the Autocrat, does not offer personal loyalty, or has a disrespectful attitude toward the Autocrat's eccentricities. On the other hand, if the seller can be "adopted" by the Autocrat, a win-win "uncle/nephew" relationship can develop.

DECISION MAKERS WHO MAKE DIFFICULT PARTNERS

There are seven types of decision makers who have low partnering potential. Figure 12 summarizes their principal characteristics and most probable negotiating modes.

The Machiavellian. It is not necessarily true that Machiavellians are unethical. They generally do not let ethics enter their negotiations. While they can be extremely ethical when it suits their purposes, they are basically cynical about people. Machiavellians depersonalize others. They can therefore concentrate on winning regardless of the loss incurred by their adversaries. Emotional considerations mean little. Machiavellians never get emotionally involved while negotiating. They use power, always seeking to augment it, and exploit others only when it is necessary.

As strategists, Machiavellians tightly control their be-

Figure 12. Low-partnering-potential decision makers.

MANAGER TYPE	CHARACTERISTICS	NEGOTIATING MODES
Machiavellian	Self-oriented, shrewd, devious, calculating, manipulative, excellent insight into people's weaknesses, opportunistic, flexible, ranges from apparent collaboration to pitiless aggression, cold but can be charming.	Treats people as things to be exploited and outwitted. Cooperates only for selfish advantage. Personal considerations do not enter into thinking. Tough, pressing strategist. Difficult negotiator. Must win at any price, in any way possible.
Missionary	Overly concerned with people and their opinions, subjective in people orientation, likable but tries too hard to be liked, excellent interpersonal skills but does not win respect, insists that conflict and friction be smoothed over.	A soft manager who prizes harmony above all else. Low task orientation. Gets emotionally involved. Acts on a personal basis. Poor strategist and weak negotiator. Tends to do what is popular. Inclined to ignore harder organizational requirements.
Exploitive Autocrat	Arrogant, self-insistent, abusive, demeaning, coercive, vindictive, domineering, often quite competent, rigid, prejudiced, given to snap judgments, exploits others' weaknesses.	Exerts constrictive personal controls. Flogs and flails anyone who is vulnerable. Uses pressure and fear to get things done. Demands subservience. High task orientation. People are seen as minions. Harsh strategist and bludgeoning negotiator.
Temporizer	Procrastinating, compromising, vacillating, always complaining, feels helpless, has strong fear of being put upon, survival instincts may be superior, usually politically aware.	Low task orientation and low people concern. Responds to the strongest immediate pressure. Reactive, not active. Inconsistent negotiator bending to heaviest pressure.

Figure 12 (continued).

MANAGER TYPE	CHARACTERISTICS	NEGOTIATING MODES
Climber	Striving, driving, energetic, self-oriented, often smooth and polished, masks aggression, unusually opportunistic, always plotting the next move or maneuver, no loyalty to organizations or people, often quite competent, "fronts" constantly.	High political skills. Excellent at maneuvering into the limelight. Predatory toward weaker managers. Welcomes and initiates self-propelling change. Uses high task orientation for self-serving purposes. Adroit with people but no interest in them. Good but tricky strategist. Self-serving negotiator.
Conserver	Status quo defender, resistant to change and innovation, seeks security, unambitious, often a skillful tactician and knowledgeable about the organization's nooks and crannies, knows how to use the system to his own best personal advantage; selfishly safeguards personal status and prerogatives.	Likes to impose a sense of order, structure, and predictable sequence. Modest task and people orientation. Self-protective strategist; often a clever obstacle builder. Defensive negotiator and may be excellent at undermining change.
Glad-Hander	Superficially effusive, deceptively friendly, extroverted, socially skilled, excellent interpersonal skills, an adept politician, superior survival instincts, fluent, humorous, but may lack substance.	Sells self-image very well. Low or modest task orientation. Unconcerned with people but excellent in dealing with them. Gets by on personality. May be clever strategist but is an inconsistent negotiator. May use people, even knife them in the back, but most often does not threaten them.

havior. They lie plausibly and they are experts at appearing to be innocent. They prefer ambiguous and unstructured situations, suspect the motives of others, and have little faith in human nature. While they resist being influenced, they are superior at influencing. Accordingly, negotiating with them is a tough, hard-nosed task. Accommodation and compromise are perceived as weaknesses. Machiavellians press to get all they can from every relationship. Trade-offs are a distasteful last resort.

The Missionary. Missionaries are at the opposite end of the continuum from Machiavellians. They are overly concerned with people, their feelings and reactions. Good human relations, harmony, and intimacy are their criteria for negotiation. Confrontation and conflict are to be avoided. Missionaries often win popularity contests but less regularly win respect. Their strategies are almost always interpersonal in nature. Negotiation means reaching agreement or delaying it in a pleasant manner. As a result, the seller may be uncertain about when an agreement will be finalized. A negative reaction will be communicated as sweetly as a positive one.

The Exploitive Autocrat. Exploiters are arrogant, harsh, and vengeful. They demand subservience. Ruling by threats and fear, Exploiters assume that sellers are inert incompetents who must be driven to do an acceptable job. This is McGregor's Theory X manager in the extreme. Negotiating with Exploiters is difficult. The seller must approach them with tactful firmness. Limits beyond which the seller cannot be pushed must be established. Exploiters consider the exploited to be weak; weakness is a vice. Sellers must be ready to encounter exploiters on their own terms: strength for strength, forcefulness for forcefulness.

The Temporizer. Temporizers never let others know where they stand. One reason may be that they do not know themselves. They are notorious responders to pressure. Because they have few convictions, they are likely to shift opinions and ideas in erratic fashion. The seller's task is not only to deal with a Temporizer but also to analyze the organizational fields of force to which the Temporizer is sensitive and reactive. The seller may be able to use these force fields to impel Temporizers to come to decisions.

The Climber. Climbers ceaselessly seek opportunities for self-advancement at the expense of anyone who happens to be vulnerable. Their loyalty, like that of Machiavellians, is solely to themselves. They use and abuse negotiating situations to propel themselves toward power and status. Climbers use aggressive strategies against the weaker and defensive strategies against those who attempt to constrain them. When blocked, Climbers are swift to move laterally. Whereas a Machiavellian may be content to be the power behind a throne, Climbers insist on being front and center. Sellers must be wary lest Climbers use them. Climbers can also help sellers climb. But identification with a Climber may invite hostility for the seller, particularly from other Climbers.

The Conserver. Conservers are hoarding types. They are basically stand-patters and status quo defenders. Anything new disturbs a Conserver. Since they have usually gone as far as they are likely to go in their company, Conservers are generally jealous of whatever status, prerogatives, and authority they possess. In contrast to the Machiavellian, the Climber, and the Exploiter, who can become a seller's helpers and recommenders, Conservers are almost always hinderers. They are ever alert to safeguarding their positions and they may be highly adept in throwing obstacles in the seller's way. Sabotage of innovative change is their forte.

The Glad-Hander. Glad-Handers are marketing personalities. Sociable, infinitely adaptable, extroverted, and superficially friendly, Glad-Handers are also unprincipled. They are incapable of lasting loyalty. They see themselves as salable commodities who are for hire to the highest bidder. Yet they are charming and personable, possessing a high degree of social skills. Sellers may be taken in at first by Glad-Handers because of their polished social veneer. But Glad-Handers do not wear well, especially under pressure. Partnering with Glad-Handers is a futile endeavor, but they can often be helpful in running interference to reach decision makers.

9

Prescription

Product sales representatives are taught to overcome customer objections. They fight them, deny them, or ignore them. Systems sellers must encourage objections. Objections are a customer's expressions of needs. For this reason, objections give precious information to the seller. They provide entry points into customer thinking. They are one of the most important ways a customer can provide "openers." The best strategy for closing them is to seek out the needs that give rise to the objections and then to meet those needs by means of system benefits.

The systems seller's response to customer objections will eventually become apparent in the system that is prescribed. Prescribing is the seller's finest art. Good systems sellers are first-rate prescribers. They size up customer needs and specify the most cost-efficient systems to benefit them.

The ability to prescribe the right system the first time is a result of three factors. One is the seller's experience. The second is the seller's expertise. The third factor is the seller's skill in solving customer business problems and helping capitalize on opportunities: in other words, helping a customer improve profit.

A system's combined advantage is expressed as a single benefit: profit improvement of the customer's process in which the system is installed. This benefit is a partial function of system price. It is also a function of the system's return on investment. The ability of a system to yield a return on investment that exceeds price endows it with premium-price capability.

Prescribing a system's package and pricing it are the two most demanding tasks of systems selling. Prescribing the package determines the customer's value and the seller's profit from the system. So does pricing the package. Because they have such a direct effect on both value and profit, the acts of prescription and pricing are the keystones of the systems seller's proficiency.

The standard of performance for prescribing and pricing a system is met when the prescription is so responsive to customer needs for improved profit that the sale is made on a noncompetitive basis and the system's premium price is accepted as proof of its added value in meeting customer objectives.

Model Systems Prescriptions

AN OFFICE COMMUNICATIONS SYSTEM

An office communications systems seller defines the business mission of office systems as improving the profit of customer word-processing functions. The communication of words back and forth in business offices is the vital customer process on which the seller's systems concentrate. To solve problems of rising communications costs and inefficiencies in communication, the seller prescribes a total communications system as opposed to the random use of a typewriter here, a dictating machine there, and a copying machine somewhere else. The system is composed of input and output processing equipment and inspection, maintenance, repair, replacement, resupply, financing, and educational services.

A FIRE PROTECTION SYSTEM

A fire protection systems seller defines the business mission of fire systems as improving the efficiency and reducing

the cost of safeguarding customer chemicals-processing functions. The refining of chemical compounds in laboratories is
the vital customer process on which the seller's systems concentrate. To solve the problem of rising cost for high-hazard
protection, the seller prescribes a total risk management system as opposed to the random use of a fire extinguisher here, a
sprinkler there, and a bucket of sand somewhere else. The
system is composed of fire detection and extinguishing equipment and inspection, maintenance, repair, replacement, resupply, financing, and educational services. Working with
these tools, the seller analyzes and defines fire protection problems from both a physical-hazard perspective and a
legislative-compliance point of view. The end objective is to be
able to insure customers against loss of business income continuity due to fire.

A MATERIALS CLEANING SYSTEM

A materials cleaning systems seller defines the business
mission of cleaning systems as improving the profit of customer electrical motor rebuilding processes. Cleaning and re-
painting electric motors is the vital customer process on which
the seller's systems concentrate. To solve the problem of rising
costs for removing dirt, grease, rust, and paint, the seller prescribes a total cleaning and finishing system as opposed to the
random use of a sandblasting machine here, a blast room there,
and steel grit abrasives somewhere else. The system is composed of blasting equipment, consumable abrasives, and related inspection, maintenance, repair, replacement, resupply,
financing, and educational services.

Responding to Customer Signals

The signal to prescribe a system comes from a customer.
It generally takes the form of a problem. There are three major
classes of customer problems that can be successfully re-
sponded to by prescribing a system:

1. A product is "too expensive" or "no better than competition."
2. A product requires "frequent servicing" or "sophisticated knowledge" to operate or maintain.
3. A product is subject to "rapid depreciation" or "technological obsolescence."

Systemizing Products That Are "Too Expensive" or "No Better than Competition"

When customers perceive a product as too expensive or no better than that of competition, the product is being classified as a commodity. The customer is positioning the product as a utility rather than as a branded specialty. Utilities are interchangeable. One supplier's utility is no better or no worse than competitive utilities. Since the only point of difference between utilities is usually the price, customers bargain with suppliers to drive price down as close as possible to cost.

Systemizing a commodity product or service can often answer the two objections of expensiveness and competitive parity. The added values offered by the system may help justify a premium price. The system may be able to deliver worthwhile benefits that the product alone cannot deliver. Thus if the system offers a preemptive benefit, its branded nature can justify a premium price even though it is built around a commodity product.

One of the most helpful components for a system to offer in order to justify price or improve on competitive value is a phased-payment financing plan that spreads out price over time. A financing plan can take the onus off a lump-sum price that is payable up front. The cost advantages of financing also act to reduce the effect of premium price. Up-front capital expenditure is avoided, allowing the customer to use otherwise sunk funds for investment purposes or other purchases. Certain tax advantages may also be possible. Finally, if the system's financing plan is presented as a service fee for use of the system's benefits rather than as a price, it may help make the system as a whole more palatable.

SYSTEMIZING PRODUCTS THAT REQUIRE FREQUENT SERVICING OR SOPHISTICATED KNOWLEDGE

When a product's normal use requires predictable periodic servicing, consumable replacement parts, or sophisticated operating knowledge, it is a natural candidate for systemizing. This situation is the perfect setting for the classic systems strategy of "the razor and the blades." The product or equipment acts as the razor. The razor is the system's hardware. It may be a one-time sale. The servicing it requires and the replacement parts and consumables act as the blades, which must be reordered through repeat sales. The blades are the system's software. Over the life cycle of the system, sale of the blades will account for the major contribution to the customer's income.

The blades also provide a second benefit. They give the systems seller continuity with customers. They offer a valid, profit-making reason to return again and again to monitor the contribution of system performance to a customer's process. This offers the opportunity to seek out new or further needs that can be supplied, maintain the product's performance so that it operates in the most cost-effective manner, and upgrade the system whenever possible with more sophisticated hardware and accessories.

A razor-and-blades system may include one, two, or all three, of the following components:

1. A periodic service agreement to provide recurrent maintenance, repair and replacement parts, and consumables.
2. An educational service to teach the customer's own personnel how to operate the system. This service may involve an intensive initial teaching program supplemented by periodic refresher courses in the form of seminars or printed and audiovisual instructional materials, or a school for customers in systems operation and maintenance.
3. An operational service that provides trained personnel

employed by the systems seller's company to run the system on a cost-plus-fee basis on the customer's premises. The seller's company provides the complete staff and handles its recruitment, compensation, motivation, and benefits.

SYSTEMIZING PRODUCTS THAT ARE SUBJECT TO RAPID DEPRECIATION OR TECHNOLOGICAL OBSOLESCENCE

When a product is subject to rapid depreciation, or if its technology can become rapidly obsolete, it may be difficult to justify a premium price.

By systemizing such a product, it can often be protected from price erosion. The system's added values add to price support. Even though a product may originally be technologically preemptive, if early obsolescence is in prospect it should be sold on the preemptive benefits of a system. This will provide the seller with a positioning that may be maintained at length. If, on the other hand, a position is based on the product's temporary technical superiority, premium-price opportunity will be lost as soon as the advantages of the product are matched by a competitor.

An extremely important component of a system designed to counter a product's depreciation or technological obsolescence is some form of leasing. If a system can be paid for over time, some of the curse can be taken off depreciation since the system's total price no longer needs to be committed at one time. This money can be invested at a return or used in other ways. Thus a lease can endow both the seller's product and the customer's capital funds with added values.

A second benefit of including a lease option in the system for a rapidly depreciating or obsolescent product is that provision can be made within the lease for periodic replacement or upgrading. These services defray the costs of obsolescence by maintaining a system in a state of modernity at all times. When a lease provides this service, it can be promoted as a service-fee method of maintaining the product's original value.

The Make-and-Buy Approach

When a systems seller prescribes a profit-improvement package, it must follow the rule of "necessity and sufficiency." All the components and services that are necessary must be included in the package. But only as many of them as will be sufficient to solve the customer's problem should be prescribed.

This guideline helps protect a seller against underengineering or overengineering a system's prescription. If a system is overengineered, it may have to be overpriced. If a system is underengineered, it may contribute to customer dissatisfaction and invite competitive inroads into the seller's account.

To avoid underengineering, the seller may have to acquire equipment or service components from other manufacturers to round out some systems. At times, it will be possible to market these components under the seller's own brand name. This is the preferred way. But even if they cannot be branded, they should nonetheless be incorporated into the system's prescription if they are necessary to enable the system to accomplish its objectives.

Building Turnover into the System Package

To be of maximum benefit to a customer and maximum profit to the seller, a system package should have turnover built into it. The package should be self-consuming. This allows a customer to maintain the system in the most modern, up-to-date manner. It also allows the seller to generate an ongoing market for the system's product-related services and consumable supplies as a means of providing continuing income and sources of growth for the seller's systems business.

A basic rule of system prescription can be stated in this way: *To maximize profit, standardize as much of the hardware as possible and customize the services and consumables.* When services and consumables are customized, a system's premium price is further justified. When frequent turnover is multiplied by premium price, maximum profits can result.

10

Packaging

Every system should be packaged with two support services. One is *customer education*. The other is *system financing*. At first glance, educating and financing may not seem to have very much in common. In systems selling, though, they form a united supportive service to the customer.

The unity of educating and financing is found in their contribution to a customer's ability to afford a system. By packaging an educational component with every system, the seller can help a customer operate a system for improved profit. By financing a customer's acquisition, the seller can help the customer afford to buy or lease a system for improved profit.

These two support elements do not simply make it easy for a customer to buy. Nor do they simply make it possible. What they should do is make it necessary. With the primary reasons for not buying displaced by the benefits of education and service-fee financing, a system should become so strongly needed by a customer that objections to it or reservations about it are overridden.

While education and financing are supportive to a system, they must not be treated as fringe benefits or sweeteners to clinch the deal. They should be positioned as integral parts of every system's benefit package.

Educating the Customer

The best system customer is the customer who has been educated in the broadest utilization of the system's potential. An educated customer knows what benefits to expect and how to achieve them. This is the customer who will appreciate a system the most because of a high level of confidence in its operation. And this is the customer who will add to and upgrade a system the most by continually setting new objectives for its performance and new applications for its operations.

A system's education component must help maximize a customer's understanding of system operations and their benefits. All systems sellers should adopt as their motto the belief that "the smarter our customers the better for us."

The need for customer education is dictated by an essential fact of systems life. The hardware expense of the average customer is generally amortized over time. Personnel costs, however, rise. By far the most money spent by customers on their systems goes not for their hard components but to their operators and appliers. A burden rests on the systems supplier to help ensure that customers achieve and maintain a high level of productivity. Customer education is the tool that underwrites the cost efficiency of a system's continuing operation.

Customer education also helps improve the profitability of the systems seller's deal. By educating customers in proper operation and maintenance of their systems, the seller takes out insurance against undue repair bills for which the seller's company may be liable under contract. The seller may also be able to avoid many customer demands for service that can come at awkward times and cause recurring unplanned and unrecoverable costs. Many sales bleed to death financially in just this way.

CREATING A CURRICULUM

A curriculum is a "system" of educational courses. It is a subsystem of the seller's total system. Its courses should be put together according to three criteria:

1. Every course should be a subject in itself. It should be able to stand alone as a comprehensive treatment of its area of study.
2. Every course should be integrated with all other courses so that the curriculum is a systematic unit rather than a loose collection of seemingly unrelated subjects.
3. The curriculum as a whole should have a measurable objective. Every course in the curriculum should have a contributing objective that is also measurable.

A customer-education curriculum for most systems will generally require a minimum of five courses. For customers in compliance industries whose processes are subject to federal, state, or local regulation, a sixth course in conforming to legislative control will also be required:

1. System operation.
2. System maintenance.
3. System financing.
4. Profit-improvement evaluation.
5. System technology.

An agenda of typical subject areas for these courses is shown in Figure 13.

INSTITUTIONALIZING THE CURRICULUM

A customer-education capability commands the greatest value as a systems component when it is institutionalized as a school. A school does far more than provide a physical place to store and distribute knowledge resources. It also acts as a symbol of the systems seller's expertise. It validates the curriculum's professionalism. A third benefit of a school is that it can function as a profit center, bringing in added income from the rental or sale of its information.

Because it represents the knowledge resource around which systems capabilities can be structured, a school may be able to play a central role in systems selling. Its existence can do more than any component other than the seller's prescrip-

Figure 13. Typical subject areas for a customer education curriculum.

System Operation Course

1. System design.
2. Operations analysis.
3. Project management.
4. Troubleshooting and problem solving.
5. Objective setting.
6. Operation monitoring.
7. Operating personnel training and development.
8. Innovative applications.

System Technology Course

1. Leading-edge technical trends and projections for system design.
2. Short-range applications of emerging technology.
3. Operational, financial, and managerial effects of new technology.

System Financing Course

1. Financing sources.
2. Lease or buy decision making.
3. Effects of financing decisions on accounting results.

Profit-Improvement Evaluation Course

1. System cost analysis.
2. Profit contribution analysis.
3. Quality contribution analysis, with specific application to sales and marketing.

System Maintenance Course

1. Preventive maintenance.
2. Repair or replacement decision making.
3. Maintenance personnel training and development.

---

tive expertise to help persuade customer acceptance. A school attests to the belief that the seller knows how to apply systems to customer businesses. This is the most important assumption that can be held on the seller's behalf since most systems customers agree that "What we're really buying is knowledge."

For a systems seller, a company school offers dual leverage. The school's knowledge can be brought to customers or customers can be brought to school. Either way, the seller will be acting as the customer's personal source of access to vital knowledge assets. IBM has organized its data processing assets into the IBM Systems Science Institute. The Institute offers leading-edge courses in systems design and management.

The Ansul Company's Fire Technology Center operates in a similar manner. Other systems suppliers have adopted an industry services institute type of school, which provides customer access to data banks and experts in management and technical services as well as marketing knowledge. An institute should be able to provide the following three knowledge resources.

Management services. An industry information data bank can help customers make more profitable decisions and solve problems in the most cost-effective manner. An institute typically accepts subscriber inquiries. It may also publish background reports that educate customers in upcoming industry trends and ways to prepare to cope with them. Periodic seminars can provide direct contact with the selling company's staff and outside experts in major knowledge areas of the industry.

Marketing services. A market research and market forecasting service can help customers formulate effective marketing strategies based on accurate knowledge of existing and emerging industry needs. An institute may conduct periodic market analysis studies and make its findings available to subscribers. Customized new-product pretest studies, buying-influence profiles, and other specific researc projects can also be accepted from subscribers for execution by the institute. Periodic seminars can provide direct contact with marketing experts and new knowledge.

Technical services. An information data bank on the technical and scientific base of historical and prospective solutions to industry problems can help customers understand the technical options open to them for new research and development projects or new-product development. An institute may conduct periodic state-of-the-art surveys and present its findings through publications and seminars. A library of product feasibility studies and systems designs can be made available for consultation and study. Technological forecasts may be undertaken on commission by corporate staff scientists and outside consultants.

Financing the Customer's System

Premium pricing is the systems seller's greatest blessing. To some customers, however, it may present a problem. In such cases, the seller has two strategies to help take the sting out of premium price. The basic strategy is always to emphasize a system's contribution to profit improvement. This directs customer attention to the benefits achievable from a system instead of the price that must be paid to receive them. The other strategy is to help the customer obtain a system's benefits by financing its acquisition.

There are three basic methods of system financing. One method is *cash flow financing.* Under this method, the seller prepares a purchase plan whose terms help the customer optimize cash flow for maximum profit improvement. For example, the customer's payments can be related to different forms of depreciation so that the system's equipment can help pay for itself. A pay-as-you-depreciate schedule allows payments to decrease over a lengthy time frame as accelerated depreciation falls and maintenance costs rise. The purchase plan can be geared to a customer's business-income cycle. For businesses affected by seasonal cycles, a deferred or skip-payment schedule can permit smaller payments or even no payments at all to be made when the customer is experiencing a low-income period.

A second method of system financing is to allow the customer to install and operate a system under a *monthly service fee,* which is payable until the system's cost is paid in full. A third method of system financing is to allow the customer to *lease* a system on a perpetual-rental basis.

While these last two methods differ, they share three similarities. Both methods permit a customer to obtain a system's benefits immediately, without the delay of having to wait until they can be afforded. Both methods substitute a series of relatively small bites of expenditure for a less easily digestible big lump. Both methods also allow the option of purchase at any time.

SERVICE-FEE FINANCING

A service-fee method of system financing lets a customer receive the service benefits of a system without the need to own the system. This is why a financing fee is called a service fee. As installments of service are received, installments of payment are made.

A service fee does away with front-end loading. The cost of a system is spread equitably over time, not dumped all at once upon purchase. The system is, in effect, leased to the customer until the final payment. At that time, full title passes. By making the payments periodic, and thereby making the sale conditional, it is often easier for the customer to acquire a system. Its essential appeal is that it enables a major expenditure to be postponed but nonetheless provides immediate service benefits. In short, service-fee financing allows a customer to have cake and eat it too.

There are two additional advantages to the service-fee method. The service fee is a time-payment or deferred-payment sale. It extends payment over time. It therefore offers a hedge against inflation. A second advantage of extending payment over time is the probability that the seller's company will upgrade the system's performance during the life of the service fee. If this occurs, a customer can benefit by taking advantage of new technical developments at no additional cost as they occur.

LEASING

Like service-fee financing, leasing is an alternative to outright purchase. Whereas service-fee financing is a form of installment buying, leasing is a form of rental. Under a lease, a customer avoids the lump-sum cost of outright purchase by renting a system. Thus the system's benefits are acquired without the necessity of ownership. In addition to the benefits of the system, a customer also benefits by conserving cash and borrowing power.

Leasing can be the preferred option for financing a system

under a wide range of conditions. Some of these conditions depend directly on the system, such as the newness of its technology, its requirements for service, or the significance of its initial cost or price premium. Other conditions depend on the size and growth stage of customer operations to be affected by a system, a customer's previous system experience, needs for continuity of service responsibility, and credit posture. The third set of conditions affecting leasing is determined by the selling situation. The most important of these situational factors are the economic cycle, inflationary pressures, legislative trends, and the policies and practices of competitive systems suppliers. Appendix 1 contains guidelines that customers use to plan and evaluate their lease/buy options.

Essentially, leasing can be an attractive alternative to purchase whenever a system's total dollar cost appears high but the profit on freed capital can outweigh the costs, and whenever assets ownership is not seen as an advantage. Some specific conditions under which leasing can be the preferred option for system financing can be summarized as follows:

Aspects of the System
1. The system's technology is new and therefore unproven, which means that a great deal of service will probably be required.
2. The system's technology is subject to rapid obsolescence, either because it is new and will incur intensive innovation or because it is old and must be significantly improved.
3. The system requires a great deal of service.
4. The system carries a high initial cost.
5. The system's price premium is significant and must be offset as much as possible by interest savings and other financial benefits of leasing.

Aspects of the Customer
1. The customer is a small or medium-size company whose cash is limited but whose cash flow is predictable.

2. The customer is experiencing rapid growth and needs to conserve capital.
3. The customer's process to be systemized is new and system application is therefore more than normally unpredictable.
4. The customer has experienced a failure from a competitive system's installation and is gun-shy.
5. The customer wants an unusually high degree and continuity of supplier responsibility.
6. The customer is fully borrowed up to the credit limit.
7. The customer wants to keep borrowing power unimpaired.
8. The customer does not want to affect the balance sheet by further borrowing.

Aspects of the Situation
1. The selling situation is characterized by accelerated technological, legislative, or economic change.
2. The economic cycle is on a downswing.
3. Inflation is on the upswing.
4. Compliance legislation affecting the customer's business requires strict ongoing system reliability.
5. Competitive systems suppliers are selling "on price" or offering unusually liberal financing terms.

The Leasing Proposal

When leasing appears to be the appropriate financing method for a systems customer, the seller will have to propose it in a manner that will emphasize its benefits. Figure 14 illustrates a model leasing proposal. Its major benefit is presented in terms of the seller's paramount promise—profit improvement. The presentation shows how profit improvement can be achieved by the ability of leasing to permit system use while conserving cash, hedging against inflation, and receiving tax advantages along with balance-sheet, operating, and accounting benefits. A model system lease is given in Appendix 2.

Figure 14. Model leasing proposal.

Profit Improvement Through Cash Conservation

The Pay-as-You-Profit Approach to System Use

Leasing is a major method of conserving cash. When you lease your system, you avoid the capital expenditures involved with ownership. Yet you obtain all the advantages of system use. Leasing allows you to benefit financially in two important ways. You get the immediate advantage of the system's profit-making capability. You also get an opportunity advantage from the working capital that you save. Because no major capital investment is required, you will be able to retain your operating funds and borrowing power. Or you can use the funds for other income-producing activities. These benefits can yield favorable effects on your cost of capital and your corporate return on investment. In many cases, your benefits can be further improved by financing the rental payments for your leased system directly out of the profits and savings it generates.

A lease enables you to put a system to work for you immediately, without delay. You can then pay for it as you profit from it. In this way, you can obtain six major types of operating and financial benefits.

1. *Profit-Improvement Benefits*

   Your profits can be improved in two ways. First, your production and processing costs can be reduced. Second, your production efficiency can be increased. This can result in higher-quality end products, fewer defects, reduced risk of callbacks and out-of-stock situations, and greater added value for your products in their markets. Not only will you be able to approach more closely the objective of zero defects; you will also improve your approach to zero complaints. A higher price, or a more securely maintained price, should result. Profit-improvement benefits can also accrue from the competitive advantage your system lets you enjoy as a lower-cost producer. Your lease also allows you to take full advantage of the output from our ongoing research and development program, whose mission is to make new cost efficiencies available to you on a continuing basis.

2. *Custom-Tailoring Benefits*

   Like your system, system lease is tailormade to your individual requirements. If your requirements change, or as you begin to perceive the full range of added values you can receive from leasing, your lease can easily be updated. After your initial lease term, you may even purchase your system.

3. *Inflation Hedging and Tax-Timing Benefits*

   Since your rental payments are made out of future pre-tax earnings, your system lease can help you hedge against inflation. By paying for your system as you profit, you can anticipate spending money of gradually decreasing value over the term of your lease. In addition, you can reduce or postpone taxes in many cases when you declare your rental payments as a deductible business expense.

4. *Off-Balance-Sheet Financing Benefits*

   Your lease may enable you to use off-balance-sheet financing. This can help conserve cash and improve your financial ratios. A lease can provide up to 100 percent financing. Terms are generally longer than loans and relieve you of the need to apply for bank credit. Furthermore, there are no compensating balance requirements. An orderly and predictable payment schedule can often be supported out of the profit improvements or cost savings your system produces.

5. *Operating and Accounting Benefits*

   Your lease can enable you to make an immediate reduction in your capital appropriations. Or it can free you to use your working capital for profitable alternative investments. Your budgeting and bookkeeping will be simplified because the lease will free you from fixed-asset accounting. Leasing also allows your system's costs, together with its contributions, to be fully predictable.

6. *Service Benefits*

   Your lease provides service benefits that help maximize the operating advantages of your system. Our service package is designed to help you achieve minimum cost for your system by assuring periodic preventive-maintenance inspection, recommendation for replacement parts, and a periodic audit of your system operations. Our applications knowledge can also play an important role in helping you integrate the system with your other operations most cost effectively.

The systems seller should be aware of some potential disadvantages to the leasing option. Off-balance-sheet financing, which allows a system to be acquired without having lease-payment obligations entered as a liability on the customer's balance sheet, may not be permitted in many cases. In these circumstances, a lease will have to be accounted for as an acquisition of property just as if it were a sale. Other possible disadvantages are:

1. The customer loses all residual rights to a system on the termination of the lease. If the customer purchases the system or renews the lease, it is with the realization that its full cost has already been amortized.

2. If interest rates decrease, the customer will nonetheless have to continue paying at the original higher rate.

3. The customer will be deprived of the tax benefits of accelerated depreciation and high interest deductions common to the early years of system ownership. These benefits would produce a temporary cash saving.

11

Pricing

For both the systems seller and a customer, problem solving means producing solutions to customer problems that have a demonstrable bottom-line dollars-and-cents effect. A problem is not considered solved until a monetary benefit can be demonstrated. The benefit may be realized by reducing a major processing cost. Or it can come from generating new revenues by increasing the capacity of a process to put out work, improving the ability of the process to operate nearer the ideal standard of zero defects, or adding a quality premium to the end product of the process so that the cost efficiency of a customer's marketing can be improved and sales demand increased.

Whether cost is reduced or new revenues are added, the benefit to the customer is the same: *profit is improved*. Profit improvement is the ultimate benefit that can be delivered by a problem-solving system. It means that the incremental investment required by system purchase or lease can return an even greater incremental profit.

Profit is generally defined as the ratio of income earned to the amount of capital invested to produce it. To improve profit, the systems seller must improve the income that a customer can earn. As the reward for improving customer profit, the seller can command a premium price that is commensurate with the degree of improvement.

Since system price depends on a customer's improved profit, system pricing is value pricing. The definition of value in terms of the amount by which profit is actually improved varies from customer to customer. As a result, there is no such fixed item as "system price" even for the same system. Price will always vary in direct proportion to the degree of value contributed by a system as measured by its return on investment, or ROI. For this reason, the systems seller will have to determine a system's ROI for every individual customer before its price can be set.

How to Price a Customer's Profit Improvement

To endow systems with a premium price, the seller must provide customers with financial justification. The dollar costs that a customer can save and the additional profits that can be earned must be quantified. By selling the system's profit improvement instead of its components, the seller provides a customer's decision makers with the rationale they need to endorse the system's required investment. Price then appears to be a function of return on investment, not a cost.

VALUING THE INCREMENT

The profit-improvement approach to pricing provides a means of valuing the benefit of a system's use in specific dollar amounts of incremental profit. It compares the profit-improvement benefits the customer can anticipate to the investment required to obtain them, including the price or rental fee for the system. Return on investment is recognized by almost all managers as the most meaningful way to measure the value that is received for each dollar that is expended. It is therefore an exceedingly persuasive selling tool.

Return-on-investment pricing is a measuring rod for evaluating the improved profit contribution that a system can make to a customer. In terms of return on investment, a customer's improved profit can be defined as the ratio of *added income earned* to the amount of the price and any other *added capital invested* in obtaining the system that produces the income.

ROI-CONNECTED PRICE

The return-on-investment basis for pricing relates price to a system's effects on the major operating and financial ingredients of profit making. Rather than base price on cost, the ROI approach connects price to the ways in which customer profit is actually measured:

1. Profit per unit of sale in dollars.
2. Turnover of operating funds.
3. The funds required to finance the operations and processes of a customer's business.
4. The total investment of capital employed, which includes a customer's working assets, plant, and facilities.

According to the return-on-investment approach to determining price, the reason a customer invests in a profit-improvement system is to earn a superior rate of return on the funds invested in it. This puts two kinds of pressure on a seller's profit-improvement proposals: (1) they must add to a customer's income, or (2) they must reduce a customer's costs.

How to Decide Which System to Propose

The return-on-investment approach is the seller's most helpful tool in determining which of two or more systems to propose to a customer as well as how to price them. A simple example will illustrate this point.

System A is forecast to improve customer sales by $200,000 and yield a profit on sales of 10 percent, or $20,000. The investment required from the customer is $100,000.

System B is forecast to improve customer sales by $300,000 and yield a profit on sales of 10 percent, or $30,000. The same $100,000 of customer investment will be required.

These two systems appear equally worthwhile in terms of their 10 percent profit yield on sales. But in terms of the return each system can achieve on the amount of customer capital it employs, System B is superior. With System B, $100,000 of capital can produce $30,000 worth of profit for a 30 percent return. System A also requires $100,000 of capital but can produce only $20,000 worth of profit for a 20 percent return.

The factor that accounts for the difference in the return on capital between the two systems is the relationship of the improved sales volume to the capital employed. System A allows its capital to turn over at the rate of 200 percent. With System B, however, the turnover is 300 percent.

Using the figures in the example, a workable shorthand formula can be used to determine return on investment:

$$\frac{\text{Profit}}{\text{Sales}} \times \frac{\text{sales}}{\text{capital employed}} = \% \text{ return on investment}$$

In the case of System A:

$$\frac{20,000}{200,000} \times \frac{200,000}{100,000} = 20\% \text{ ROI}$$

In the case of System B:

$$\frac{30,000}{300,000} \times \frac{300,000}{100,000} = 30\% \text{ ROI}$$

In this simplified approach, the first fraction helps the seller calculate the percentage of profit on sales. The second fraction calculates the turnover rate. When the two fractions are multiplied, they determine return on investment. Turnover is the multiplier of profits. Any improvement in the turnover of funds invested in a system's total assets, working assets, or any component part of an individual asset will increase turnover and therefore have a multiplying effect on profits.

The shortened formula for ROI can be simplified even

further for use as a quick screen when the seller wants to rule
out a system prescription that cannot offer superior potential:

$$\frac{\text{Profit}}{\text{Capital employed}} = \text{ROI}$$

The seller should not use this stripped-down formula for
anything more than preliminary, quick-screening purposes.
Without the ability to disclose the significance of the costs and
the level of capital employed in relation to sales volume, the
seller may limit both scope and accuracy in recommending
systems that can yield the best values.

System-Opportunity Identification

The return-on-investment approach is the seller's best
diagnostic tool to identify system opportunities. As the ROI
formula shows, a system opportunity is always present when it
can change either a customer's operating profit rate or turnover.

Figure 15 shows options open to a seller in recommending
a system that can improve turnover. By reducing the amount
of customer funds invested in receivables or inventories, for

Figure 15. Options open to improve turnover.

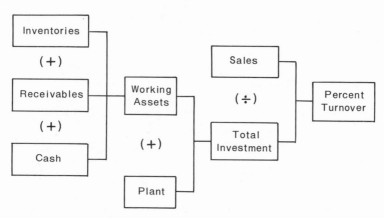

example, a system can help reduce the customer's total investment base. As a result, the system can improve the turnover of customer capital.

Figure 16 shows the options open to a seller in recommending a system that can improve operating profit. By reducing a customer's cost of sales, for example, a system can help reduce the customer's total cost structure. As a result, the system can improve customer operating profit.

Figure 16. Options open to improve operating profit.

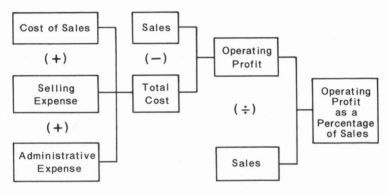

Any system option a seller recommends must meet customer standards of what constitutes an adequate return on investment. Any system whose promise of profit improvement falls below this standard will probably be rejected as not being worth the investment.

Most customers accept three standards for determining whether a given rate of return on investment is adequate: the basic cost of money, the risk, and the return for technological capabilities. The seller can apply these standards to systems options in the following manner:

1. An acceptable system must deliver a return on investment that exceeds the return on no-risk investments such as the interest rate on high-grade utility bonds, government bonds, or the prime interest rate.

2. An acceptable system must deliver a return on investment that exceeds the return on investments of equal risk.

3. An acceptable system must deliver a return on investment that fairly compensates the customer for investing in the
capabilities it requires to install and operate. These capabilities
include manpower, processing technology, product design,
patents, and general operating know-how.

The Profit-Improvement Approach to Pricing

Four successive steps make up the profit-improvement
approach to creating a price for a system.

Step 1. Work with a customer to determine profit needs
and the requirements they impose on the most cost-effective
system prescription. In response to customer needs, prescribe
the system that best meets profit-improvement requirements.
Do not quote a price. If a price is quoted in Step 1, the customer will be forced to make a decision based on competitive
system component prices or operational performance benefits.
This can reduce the system to a commodity.

Step 2. Request a profit-improvement conference with the
customer's decision makers and their influencers. During the
conference, present the system's profit-improvement contribution as the principal benefit it can deliver. Ask the customer to
provide the operating cost information needed to prepare a
profit-improvement proofbook for the customer's process that
will be systemized. Before the end of the profit-improvement
conference a date should be agreed on for a work session between the systems seller and customer representatives.

Step 3. At the work session, the customer will be
expected to share operating cost information with the seller.
If it is customer policy not to reveal hard numbers, soft
numbers in the form of estimates or ranges will be acceptable.
The seller should also be able to supply soft numbers from
access to the home office industry information base that sup-
ports systems selling. The seller will be expected to apply
profit-improvement calculations to the numbers. These calculations will primarily affect the quality, cost, or volume of the
output from a customer process. It is important that seller and
customer jointly make these respective contributions to the

profit-improvement proofbook that is the end product of their
work session so that the discovery of profit-improvement opportunities can be mutually arrived at. Before the work session
ends, seller and customer should agree on the prescribed system's ability to deliver a profit improvement and its approximate value.

Step 4. Prepare a copy of the edited profit-improvement
proofbook for customer decision makers and influencers. Reserve one copy for the home office case history library on profit
improvement. Insert the proofbook in a profit-improvement
proposal. As its name suggests, the proofbook's calculations
prove the profit-improvement benefit of the system. Price
should be based on the value of this benefit. The general rule of
ROI pricing says that price should always be lower than the
dollarized return on investing in the system but that price
should always be as high as possible under that ceiling. How
high "high" is will depend on the nature and urgency of customer need, the state of customer business, and the ability of
competitive systems suppliers to achieve similar or superior
returns on investments with their own systems.

The customer orientation of this profit-improvement approach to pricing can be seen in the summary of the capital
budgeting process that appears in Appendix 3.

The Profit-Improvement Proofbook

The seller's profit-improvement proofbook validates the
prescription of improved profit. A proofbook translates the
promise of words into numbers. It deals with four types of
analysis:

1. Incremental-investment analysis, which puts numbers
   on the added investment a customer must make to acquire a system.
2. Profit-improvement analysis, which puts numbers on
   the decreased annual operating costs or increased revenues that the system can contribute. These numbers
   provide justification for the customer's incremental investment.

3. An analysis of next year's operating benefits, which puts numbers on the proposed cost reductions and new revenues that can be expected on a comparative basis that relates next year's improvements to the status quo of the year before.
4. Return-on-investment analysis, which puts a number on the return the customer will receive for making the required investment in the seller's system.

A model proofbook is shown in Figure 17. The numbers in the model refer to a materials cleaning system whose function is to clean metal parts of rust, corrosion, and other surface imperfections as an integral part of a customer's manufacturing process. The system's equipment represents a highly visible capital outlay. Its inclusion in the system must therefore be justified by making its profit contribution equally visible. This occurs in Stage 4, where the seller has calculated the equipment's profit return on the incremental investment required to obtain it. A before-tax rate of return of over 86 percent is shown to be contributed by a $24,952 projected profit im-

Figure 17. Profit-improvement proofbook.

I. INCREMENTAL INVESTMENT REQUIRED

1. Cost of proposed equipment	$ 39,600			
Estimated installation cost	6,000			
Subtotal	$ 45,600			
Minus initial tax benefit of	3,190	Total	$ 42,410	1
2. Disposal value of equipment to be replaced	8,000			
Capital additions required in absence of proposed equipment	6,000			
Minus initial tax benefit for capital additions of	420	Total	$ 13,580	2
3. Incremental investment (1 − 2)			$ 28,830	3

(*continued*)

Figure 17 (continued).

II. PROFIT IMPROVEMENT (ANNUAL CONTRIBUTION)

4. Profit improvement-net decrease in operating costs (from line 27) $ 24,952   4

5. Profit improvement-net increase in revenue (from line 31) $ _____   5

6. Annual profit improvement (lines 4 + 5) $ 24,952   6

III. NEXT YEAR OPERATING BENEFITS FROM PROPOSED EQUIPMENT

A. Effect of Proposed Equipment on Operating Costs

(Computed on Machine-Hour Basis)	*Present*	*Proposed*	
7. Direct labor (wages, plus incentives and bonuses)	$ 10.50	$ 3.50	7
8. Indirect labor (supervisors, inspectors, helpers)	3.67	1.22	8
9. Fringe benefits (vacations, pensions, insurance, etc.)	2.15	72	9
10. Maintenance (ordinary only, parts and maintenance labor)	1.18	.90	10
11. Abrasive, media, compounds, or other consumable supplies	1.32	1.10	11
12. Power	.56	.48	12
13. Total (sum of 7 through 12)	$ 19.38	$ 7.92	13
14. Estimated machine-hours to be operated next year	2400	3000	14

(continued)

Figure 17 (continued).

15. Partial operating costs next year (13 × 14)	$ 46,512 (A)	$ 23,760 (B)	15
16. Partial operating profit improvement (15A – 15B)		$ 22,752	16

(Computed on Yearly Basis)	*Increase*	*Decrease*	
17. Scrap or damaged work	$ _____	$ 700	17
18. Downtime	_____	1500	18
19. Floor space	_____	_____	19
20. Subcontracting	_____	_____	20
21. Inventory	_____	_____	21
22. Safety	_____	_____	22
23. Flexibility			23
24. Other	_____	_____	24
25. Total	$ _____ (A)	$ 2,200 (B)	25
26. Net decrease in operating costs (partial) (25B – 25A)		$ 2,200	26
27. Total effect of proposed equipment on operating costs (16 + 26)		$ 24,952	27

B. Effect of Proposed Equipment on Revenue

(Computed on Yearly Basis)	*Increase*	*Decrease*	
28. From change in quality of products	$ _____	$ _____	28
29. From change in volume of output	_____	_____	29
30. Total	$ _____ (A)	$ _____ (B)	30
31. Net increase in revenue (30A – 30B)		$ _____	31

(continued)

Figure 17 (continued).

IV. Return on Incremental Investment

32. Incremental investment (line 3)	$ 28,830	32
33. Annual profit improvement (line 6)	$ 24,952	33
34. Before-tax return on investment (line 33 ÷ line 32)	% 86.55	34

provement. When this figure is compared against the incremental investment of $28,830 demanded by the system's equipment, the actual dollar amount involved in the transaction is greatly diminished. Even more important, the rate of return it promises becomes the focal point of the sale.

As the figure shows, the seller has taken three stages to get to the point where a number can be put on the value contributed by the system's hardware. At Stage 1, the total incremental investment required by purchase and installation of the system's equipment is itemized. Stage 2 sets down the annual contribution to profit improvement that the seller believes the system's equipment can make. Sometimes this contribution will take the form of a net increase in revenue. In this case it comes from a net decrease in operating costs. As the seller shows in Stage 3, these decreased operating costs can be expected to come largely from a decrease in customer downtime as well as reduced scrap or damaged work. They will also be derived from reduced costs of labor, fringe benefits, maintenance, and power.

A shorter format for calculating a system investment's return is the costs-benefits analysis shown in Figure 18.

Premium Price as the Conditioner of Premium Value

In systems selling, premium price is not a burden. It serves as documentation of a system's value. A premium price

Figure 18. Costs-benefits analysis.

Incremental Investment

1. Cost of proposed equipment $ _____
2. *Plus:* Installation costs   _____
3. *Plus:* Investment in other assets required   _____
4. *Minus:* Avoidable costs (repairs and re-
             modeling)   _____
5. *Minus:* Net cash proceeds after tax ad-
             justment for sale of properties re-
             tired as a result of investment   _____
6. *Minus:* Investment credit (if applicable)   _____
7. Total investment (sum of 1–6)   _____

	A. Present or Competitive	B. Your Proposal	C. ± Difference
Cost Benefit (Annual Basis)			
8. Sales revenue (may be zero)	$____	$____	$____
9. *Minus:* Variable costs:			
10. Labor (including fringe benefits)	____	____	____
11. Materials	____	____	____
12. Maintenance	____	____	____
13. Other variable costs	____		____
14. Total variable costs (10–13)	____	____	____
15. Contribution margin (8–14)	____	____	____
16. *Minus:* Fixed costs:			
17. Rent or depreciation on equipment	____	____	____
18. Other fixed costs	____	____	____
19. Total fixed costs (17 + 18)	____	____	____
20. Net income before taxes (15 − 19) *	____	____	____

* If tax rate is known, calculate on after-tax basis.

(*continued*)

Figure 18 (continued).

Accounting Rate of Return on Proposed Investment

   21. Total investment cost (line 7) $ _____

   22. Average net income before taxes
       (line 20) *   _____

   23. Before-tax rate of return
       (line 22 ÷ line 21) †

* If tax rate is known, calculate on after-tax basis.
† Average annual net income over life of the investment.

---

documents premium value. It makes claims of systems performance believable. It justifies the promise of close, continuing service support to buttress the system's operation. And it assigns a numerical value to the system's essential component: the seller's prescriptive expertise and the ability to apply it to a customer's business.

The systems seller must aggressively promote a system's premium value of profit improvement as the validation of its price. Unselling price is not the problem. Selling profit improvement is the nature of the task.

By raising an umbrella of premium price over a system, the seller requires customers to focus their decision making on value. Instead of being defensive about price, the seller must use price to alert customers to expect unusual value. Price is a conditioner. It conditions the seller to overcome price dread and encourages an aggressive positioning of systems around added values instead of apologetically around added costs.

To use price as a conditioner of the expectation of premium value, the seller must reverse the usual defensive presentation of price, which says: "My system is high-priced. But it delivers premium value." Instead, price should be presented as follows: "My system carries a premium price. *Therefore* you can expect premium value from it." In this way, price loses its liability. It becomes the reason why added value is obtainable as well as proof that added value is embedded in the system.

Avoiding "Overpricing"

By offering significant added value, the systems seller can escape the need to be the lowest-price supplier or even a parity pricer. If the value of a system's profit-improvement benefit can be positioned at a premium level, the opportunity is created for premium pricing. Only when the "premium value, premium price" relationship becomes mismanaged will the systems seller encounter the objection of being overpriced.

The seller runs the risk of being accused of overpricing in one or more of the following three circumstances:

1. A customer's needs are incorrectly perceived and so the seller prescribes the wrong system to benefit them. Any price is too high a price for the wrong system.

2. A system is overengineered either because customer needs have been incorrectly perceived or the seller has become distracted from the mission to provide the best benefit and instead provides the most components. In either of these situations, the system will lack the value of custom-tailoring. This will make its value-to-price relationship too low and its price perceived as correspondingly too high.

3. The customer is not convinced of the premium value of the seller's prescriptive and applications expertise. The system will then be evaluated on the basis of the comparative price of its components. The price may be called too high when, in reality, it is the added value of the seller's systems-management capability that is perceived as being too low.

12

Presentation

Presentation, both written and oral, is a systems seller's principal selling tool. A systems presentation has two objectives. One is to *educate*. As a teaching tool, the presentation prepares a customer to anticipate the system's profit-improvement benefit. The second objective is to *motivate*. The presentation must stimulate a customer to want to possess the system's benefit.

System presentation is a four-step process: definition of the present financial impact of a customer problem to be solved or a customer opportunity to be capitalized on; prescription of the profit-improvement benefit from solving the problem or capitalizing on the opportunity; description of the operational and financial workings of the system that can yield the improved profit; and implementation of a control procedure to assure progress in partnership with the customer.

Step 1: Problem/Opportunity Definition

The systems seller's initial task is to establish credibility. Initial credibility comes only from displaying knowledge of a customer's business. Until a customer can say, "The salesperson knows my business," the customer will rarely be inclined to say, "That salesperson can sell me a system."

As far as systems selling is concerned, the seller must be knowledgeable about two areas of a customer's business. First, the seller must know the location of significant cost centers in one of a customer's major functions, processes, or operations that are susceptible to reduction by the seller's systems capability. Second, the seller must know how a customer's customers can be induced to buy more from the customer so that the systems customer will buy more systems capability from the seller. In the first instance, the seller must prescribe a system that will reduce customer costs. This is a problem-solving system. In the second instance, the seller must prescribe a system that will increase customer sales. This is an opportunity-seizing system.

Defining a customer problem or opportunity has two parts: what the seller knows and how the seller knows it. The second part documents the first by citing the sources of the seller's knowledge. It also reinforces the seller's credibility.

There are three likely sources of a seller's knowledge about the existence and extent of a customer cost problem or sales opportunity. The seller can know about it because the customer has revealed it. This is the "horse's mouth" source. The seller's knowledge can come from past experience with the customer, with other companies in the same industry, or with companies in a similar industry. This source is the seller's "track record." Or the seller's knowledge can come from homework. This is the "midnight oil" source.

Step 2: Profit-Improvement Prescription

The objective of the first step in a system presentation is to say to a customer, in effect: "Look here. You have a situation that is detrimental to your profit. Either you are incurring unnecessary costs or you are failing to capture available sales revenues." The objective of the presentation's second step is to say, "I can help you reduce some of those costs or gain some of those sales at a cost-beneficial investment."

In this way, the seller further reinforces the perception of being knowledgeable about the customer's business by framing the system's benefit in businesslike terms of return on investment. By quantifying an added value the system can make to the customer's operations, the seller is creating a business-manager-to-business-manager context for customer decision making.

The seller's prescription for customer profit improvement must specify the positive return that can predictably be forthcoming from installation of the seller's system. The return should be specified as both a percentage rate of improvement and its equivalent in dollars. These quantifications, the end-benefit specifications in money terms, rather than system operating performance specifications or component specifications, are the ultimate specifications of the seller's system. These are what a customer will or will not buy. They are therefore what the seller must prescribe for delivery.

Step 3: System Definition and Price Justification

The third presentation step is to define the "solution system" that will deliver the promised profit-improvement benefit and to justify its premium price by interpreting price in return-on-investment terms. In the language of systems presentation, customers are not asked to buy systems. They are invited to improve profit. They are not quoted a system's price. They are promised a positive return on the price of their system, which allows it to be treated as an investment, a cost that pays back more than is paid out.

The purpose of defining the system is not to sell it. Rather, it is to present the hardware and software package as a form of proof that the promised benefit has substance and that it is derived from known capabilities that have been prescribed by the seller precisely because they will contribute in the most cost-beneficial way to the customer's profit improvement. The system substantiates the seller's promise. Its capabilities, plus the seller's management expertise in applying them, are the means of conferring new profitability on the customer.

Price is an intimate part of a system. It is the single most revealing component. Not only does it have high visibility. It also possesses high connotative power. Premium price connotes premium value. It conveys more than the system's cost. It communicates the system's value.

Premium price can be justified by a system's ability to deliver premium value. If price contributes to value by assuring a system's quality, and if price can be recovered by a return on investment that exceeds it, price can be justifiably set at a premium level.

The third step in the system presentation process is always the most complex and often the most cumbersome. A system's hardware and software must be laid out. Their component-by-component contributions to a positive return may be itemized. The system's price requires translation into a contribution to return on investment. Yet when all is said and done, the complexity and cumbersomeness of the third step is only a footnote—albeit a necessary one—to the customer profit improvement promised in Step 2.

Price documents the system's value. The system itself documents the systems seller's promised benefit. These two attributes of tme system presentation process highlight the distinctions between commodity product selling and systems selling. In product selling, the product itself is pushed for sale, not its contribution to customer profit. Price is a detriment, not an asset. It is perceived as a sunk cost to a customer and not a recoverable benefit. It is often apologized for and may be justifiable only if the product's sale is padded with free goods or services that effectively lower it. In systems selling, there can be justifiable pride in price.

Step 4: Partnership Control Procedure

The final step in a system's presentation is to set down the standards by which the seller will progressively monitor the system's ability to deliver the promised benefit in partnership with the customer. At least three control standards should be set so that a working partnership can be confirmed between seller and customer:

1. Time frames for the accomplishment of each installation and operational stage.
2. Checkpoints for measuring the impacts of phasing the system into customer processing functions.
3. Periodic progress review and report sessions to head off problems and anticipate new applications and opportunities for system extension, upgrading, modernization, and replacement.

A model system presentation outline, which approximates this four-step format, is shown in Figure 19 on the following pages. As a system proposal of this type is progressively presented, it should make successive alterations of a customer's propensity to buy. Defining a customer problem or opportunity should condition a customer to relate to the seller as a business manager. Selling systems is a business proposition because it affects profit, the bull's-eye business objective. The next presentation step, prescribing a quantified benefit, should condition a customer to regard the system as a profit-making investment, not as a cost or a collection of components. Defining the system and justifying its price should condition a customer to credit the seller's promise as believable and achievable. Partnership in applying controls should condition the customer to accept the seller as a co-profit improver who will work cooperatively within common standards of performance, apply common yardsticks to measure progress, and accept common sharing of the workload.

Figure 19. A proposal to improve the profit of Trickle River Canyon Power Company.

CHASTE WASTECORP

(1) Problem to Be Solved

Cost-effective disposal of low-level radioactive waste.

(2) Prescription to Solve the Problem

Improve profit by reducing annual costs of handling low-level radioactive waste by more than $400,000 and simultaneously maintain complete safety together with full legislative compliance.

(3.1) Solution System

1. AECC volume-reduction system

1.1 Handles all plant-generated liquid wastes.

1.2 Twenty to fifty gallons per hour; will handle a two-unit plant.

1.3 Produces dry free-flowing product.

1.4 Automatic, remote operation including system. Decontamination for maintenance.

1.5 Non-mechanical fluid bed dryer.

2. Licensability * consultation services

3. Technical support services

3.1 Inspection of equipment during storage—refurbishment if required.

3.2 Live-in engineering consultation during installation.

3.3 Training of operating and maintenance personnel.

3.4 Live-in engineering consultation during startup.

3.5 Engineering participation during demonstration test.

4. Equipment supply contract services

5. Maintenance contract services

6. Total project management consultation service to concentrate single-source responsibility provided by Mr. Howard Berrian

7. Access to our information bank on radiation-waste disposal

(*continued*)

* Topical Report AECC-1-A; approved by NRC, December 1975.

Figure 19 (continued).

(3.2) Solution System Rate of Return

Accounting rate of return	=	29.2%
Cost savings/year	=	+$400,000

Incremental Investment

Cost of equipment	$1,000,000
Installation	200,000
Building space penalty	200,000
Total cost	$1,400,000

Operating Costs (Dollars in $000)

Costs	Present System	Proposed System
Labor	$120	$ 25
Material	200	11
Transportation and burial	280	70
Maintenance	20	30
Power	1	20
Depreciation	40	96
Totals	$661	$252

Proposed Annual Savings = $409,000

$$\frac{409,000}{661,000} = 61.9\% \text{ Cost reduction benefit}$$

Profitability Evaluation

Accounting Rate of Return

Total investment	$1,400,000	
Annual savings before tax	409,000	
Annual savings after 48% tax	212,000	
Rate of return		15.1%

Cash-Flow Payback (W/O Escalations)

1. Savings after tax = $212,000 per year
2. Straight-line depreciation (4% per year) = $56,000
3. Investment-tax credit (10%) = $140,000 (2nd year)
   Cash payback by end of 5th year (4 years, 9 months)

(*continued*)

Figure 19 (continued).

(4) Trickle River Canyon Power Company/Chaste Wastecorp Partnership
1. Personal, consultative management by Mr. Howard Berrian in close, continuing partnership with Trickle River Canyon management.
2. Thirty-day progress-review meetings.
3. Follow-on planning to optimize Trickle River Canyon investment into the future.

13

Planting

As soon as a system is in place and can be shown to be producing the profit improvement that has been prescribed for it, follow-on selling should begin. This is because the best system customer is the system user. The heavier the use, the better the customer.

Installing a system should therefore be regarded as planting the seed for follow-on sales opportunities, not the end of the sale. Once a sale has been made, the systems seller has acquired a major asset: a satisfied customer. The seller can satisfy the customer even further by promising additional profit improvement through one or more of three types of follow-up. The seller can offer to supplement the initial system with added components. Perhaps some components may have been sacrificed for financial reasons at the time the original system was approved. Or perhaps the need has become apparent only after installation. As a second type of follow-up, the seller can offer to *upgrade* the original components, up to and including the ultimate upgrading, which is total replacement of the system. Or third, the seller can offer to *integrate* an entirely new complementary system with the initial system.

These follow-up sales opportunities are not mutually exclusive. On many occasions, a seller can use all three approaches in sequence with the same customer. First, the seller can supplement the customer's system. Then, at a later date, some of the original components can be upgraded. Finally, a complementary new system can be integrated with the original one. Then the sales approach can be recycled over and over again by offering to supplement the new system, then upgrade it, and eventually integrate a third system with the first two. This recycling strategy can be illustrated in the following manner.

After an initial system is in place and producing prescribed profit-improvement benefits:

Cycle 1
1. Supplement initial system with add-on components.
2. Upgrade components of initial system with technically innovated products or equipment.
3. Integrate a complementary new system with the initial system.

Cycle 2
1. Supplement new system with add-on components.
2. Upgrade components of new system with technically innovated products or equipment.
3. Integrate a second complementary system with one or the other existing system.

Cycle 3
Repeat Cycle 2, and so on.

Supplementing an Original System

Many systems are sold lean. They are constructed of only minimum components. Or every individual component offers just the minimum performance required to deliver a customer's profit improvement. Sometimes both conditions exist. They come about because it is often easier for the systems seller to sell a minimal system. A minimal system may be the only system that survives a desystemizing process. In such cases, the initial sale contains the planting opportunity for follow-on sales.

Supplementary components, either add-ons or components with greater performance or service values, must be offered in exactly the same customer-targeted way as the original system. They must be sold on their ability to contribute added profit improvement over and above their cost.

Upgrading Original Components

The systems seller's technology-support capability is a major sales point. Customers expect to become its beneficiaries. It is also one of the seller's major cost components. It adds to price. For both reasons, the seller must pay off on technical ability by upgrading a system's original components on a progressive, periodic basis. The ultimate upgrading, of course, is the replacement of an entire system by an upgraded one.

Technological innovation almost always raises the cost of a system's equipment. Accordingly, it must also raise the equipment's ability to improve customer profit. Under a leasing agreement with a customer, provision may exist for incorporating newly improved products and equipment into a customer's system without imposing an additional fee. When customers operate under a purchase agreement, trade-ins of original equipment can make it easy for them to obtain upgraded components.

Free modifications with upgraded components can create customer good will. They may also encourage a customer to make increased use of a system's equipment in order to derive the benefits of faster, better performance. If a system uses consumables, their use will increase also. In addition to improving revenues, upgrading may also be able to generate important cost reduction benefits for the seller. The optimal life of a system's equipment may be extended by several years. If the equipment has already been totally amortized, substantial savings can accrue. Furthermore, costly service calls and repairs can be greatly reduced once upgraded equipment is installed. In these ways, the annual return on conversion cost can be at the 50 percent or higher level.

Integrating a Complementary System

Systems are designed to improve the profit of a specific process or, more typically, a specific operational system within a process. Once a system begins to deliver benefits to an operating process, the potential for achieving similar benefits in closely related or interacting operations may become apparent. In such a case, the systems seller is in an excellent position to recommend a complementary new system that can be integrated with the customer's initial system.

The seller must be careful to sell the new system on its own merits as a profit-improver. It must not be treated as a bonus for the customer's investment in the original system. This means that the new system's specific contribution to profit and cost should be carefully spelled out, along with its service requirements and operating peculiarities. If it cannot stand on its own in this way, it should not be recommended. The reason for this caution is simple to explain: It is based on the double-or-nothing principle.

While it is true that the best customer for a new system is an existing customer, the seller can just as easily lose two sales as make two. If the second system fails to deliver the promised benefits, both systems become at risk. The second system's problems will almost inevitably contaminate the original system. Even though the initial system continues to deliver improved profit, it can become at risk if its most vital component, the systems seller's personal expertise, comes into question.

If the complementary system will yield a lower profit improvement than the original system, the seller must say so. If the complementary system has a lower or slower yield or a shorter expected life cycle than the original system, the seller must also say so. Only if each complementary system carries its own justification can the seller ensure customer relations against an epidemic of serial no-confidence in the event of a single failure.

Referral Selling from Installed Systems

An existing customer is the best reference for a new customer. Systems selling is inescapably referral selling. Every new customer wants to see the benefits from an operating system that is similar to what the seller will prescribe or that is solving a similar problem. Essentially, a customer wants to see the system's added values at work. In this way, the customer comes to "realize" it; that is, to perceive it as real. The customer also wants to hear a disinterested third party rather than the seller testify about the system's benefits under actual operating conditions.

Systems selling therefore represents a highly unusual selling situation. For one thing, a new customer wants an existing customer to become a seller of the system. The new customer wants the system's claims of profit-improvement benefits to be validated. Few other sales situations are so strongly dependent on another customer's selling ability.

The second unusual characteristic of systems selling is that the traditional roles of seller and customer are reversed. From a new customer's point of view, the existing customer becomes "the seller." It is the existing customer's benefit story that is listened to. The systems seller becomes the "reference," referring the new customer to the existing customer. The less active the role the seller plays beyond that, the better.

Since the seller cannot survive without testimonial references from satisfied customers, every customer should be educated to play the role of reference as soon as the customer achieves satisfaction from a system's benefits. By teaching a customer how to verbalize benefits, the seller is practicing the principle of reinforcement. This principle says that the best way to learn something is to teach it. By teaching a new customer how a system works and what its benefits are, an existing customer can very quickly become familiar with them.

To become an accomplished reference, the systems seller will have to learn how to educate customers to be witnesses. The seller should maintain a case history testimonial portfolio to store witnessed solutions to similar problems, similar systems, and the seller's record of accomplishment in helping customers achieve their planned profit-improvement benefits.

Planting Future Reference Seeds

Every customer is a former prospect. In a systems seller's terms, a prospect is a student who is being educated to become a long-term customer. The main part of customer education is to convey what profit-improvement benefits and other advantages can be expected from one of the seller's systems once it is acquired. A secondary part of customer education is to encourage the customer to become a good reference for the system by observing how other customers carry out the role.

When a systems seller introduces a prospect to the first customer who will attest to a system's benefits, the moment should be seized to teach lesson number one in customer responsibility. "Every one of my customers," the seller must make clear, "was at one time a prospective customer just like you are today. They very properly required, as you are doing now, the opportunity to inspect the benefits of a similar system, or a system that is solving similar problems or achieving similar levels of profit improvement. My customers are proud to act as references for their systems. I don't ask them to do this as a favor to me. Quite the contrary, they and I agree that we all share a responsibility to communicate helpful information that will enable others to operate their key processes more profitably. I am sure you will feel the same way when you have validated the profit benefits from your forthcoming system."

In this way, the seller can plant the seeds for future referencing that is not looked upon as a personal favor but as an industry responsibility. The seller also instills faith and confidence in a prospective customer's mind about the expected success of a system. At the same time, a customer receives a preview of forthcoming pride in system accomplishment.

In order to keep a referral sales strategy professionally sharp, the systems seller should maintain a record of reference seeds containing the names of every customer who can reference one or more systems, the names of every customer's decision makers who have committed themselves to act as references, the prospective customers who have been referred to them or will be referred to them in the future, and the dates of every reference. By consulting a reference seed planter, a seller will be able to tell at a glance what referrals have been made, to whom, and with what frequency over the most recent period of time. The seed planter will prevent the unintentional overuse of certain references and, in addition, will allow the practice of referencing to be spread across a broad, representative range of customers.

Two Valuable Tools: Proposals and Testimonials

The systems seller has two valuable planting tools. One is the profit-improvement proposal, which prescribes new profits for customers. The second is the case history testimonial portfolio, which helps the seller validate profit-improvement proposals by documenting actual new profit achievements. The combination of these two tools equips the seller with promise and proof.

The seller should start on the preparation of a case history testimonial portfolio as soon as the profit-improvement objectives of the first system installation begin to be achieved. The portfolio should be updated as every customer's installation produces its profit contribution. In this way, the portfolio will always be current.

There are three forms in which the portfolio's information should be kept. One is a *problem inventory*. This will give the seller a proofbook of track records in solving problems that are classified according to the nature of each problem. It will enable the seller to be instantly responsive to the customer question, "Do you have experience with my kind of problem?"

The second form is a *system inventory* of solutions to customer problems. This will give the seller a proofbook of track records in solving problems that are classified according to type of system. It will enable the seller to be instantly responsive to the customer question, "Do you have experience with this type of system?"

The third form is a *profit-improvement inventory* of the dollar amounts and percentages of new profits the seller's systems have enabled customers to earn. This will give the seller a proofbook of solutions that are classified according to improvements brought to customer profit. It will enable the seller to be instantly responsive to the customer question, "Do you have experience in improving profit to this degree?"

14

Protection

A systems seller's prescription for improved customer profit is always threatened by desystemizing. The seller should not fear the process. It plays the vital role of confirming the value of the seller's prescriptive expertise and the ability to apply it to a customer's problems.

The seller's essential value is the ability to *apply*. This is what a system's prescription really is—an application of the seller's capabilities.

To this extent, the systems seller is an applications consultant. All the professional expertise in the world is valueless unless the seller can apply it to improve a customer's profit. By protecting a prescribed system against customer attempts to desystemize it, the seller learns the extent of the customer's perceived value of the seller's prescriptions and applications skills.

Challenges to desystemize a system are actually a customer's attempt to test the worth of a seller's applications expertise, which is the seller's trump card to justify premium price. Desystemizing is a price-reduction strategy. Since premium price lies at the heart of systems selling strategy, the system must be protected if premium price is to be maintained.

A system is only as good as its seller's applications ability. Unless the seller's expertise can be *branded*—that is, accepted as providing a value that exceeds its price and that is uniquely obtainable from the seller—a system cannot be protected from customer attempts to desystemize it.

There are two basic desystemizing strategies that customers practice in order to threaten the unity of systems:

1. Attempts to acquire only certain components of a system.
2. Attempts to acquire only the seller's prescriptive expertise and information base.

Protecting Against the Two Major Threats

When a customer threatens to desystemize a system, the seller has recourse to two types of strategy. One is the "yes strategy," which is defensive against the only-certain-components attack. The other is the "no strategy," which is defensive against the only-the-prescription-and-information-components attack.

"Yes Strategy"

A customer who does not want to pay the premium price for a complete system but who still sees value in obtaining some of its components will try to pick and choose. This is often like the Chinese-restaurant strategy of selecting one from column A and one from column B. When a system is attacked in piecemeal fashion, the best protective strategy for the seller to adopt in most cases is to say yes. There are three reasons:

1. *The seller makes a sale.* A partial sale is usually better than no sale at all. At least some income is earned to pay off a portion of the sales cost. The seller's morale is also boosted.

2. *The seller has a foot in the door.* Even a partial sale gets the seller involved with a customer. This gives the seller the opportunity to apply upgrading sales strategies that can gradually supply the system with additional components. This is the way many partial systems become full systems. In most businesses, customers tend to stick with their original system

suppliers. Up to 90 percent of many systems sales come from add-on purchases by existing customers.

3. *The seller can add new industry information.* Every customer problem that is solved yields new information about the customer and the customer's industry. A new cost center may be found. A new way of reducing it may be discovered. A new sales opportunity may be identified. A new way of seizing it may be tried. Every sales opportunity should be evaluated on the basis of its ability to add these new kinds of knowledge. The sum total of the added values of new learning becomes the seller's experience.

From these three reasons for saying yes to a selective customer, it is apparent that the seller's agreement to selling part of a system must be tempered by one consideration. No matter what components are agreed on, the seller's prescriptive expertise in profit-improvement planning and the information base on which it depends must always be included in the sale. A seller's recommended responses are tabulated below

System Components	Recommended Seller's Responses to Customer Desystemizing
Swing table, blast-cleaning machine, and worktable	Yes
Operating supplies, including steel grit abrasives, and replacement parts	Yes
Environmental control: fabric filter dust collector to prevent in-plant and outside air pollution	Yes
Operating personnel training program on cost-effective operation and maintenance	Yes
Periodic inspection and maintenance-monitoring service	Yes
Profit-improvement planning service to reduce cost and improve profit from materials cleaning process	No
Customer information service on applying new developments in the technology of blast cleaning, equipment, components, and supplies	No

for each of seven desystemizing attempts against a materials cleaning system. According to the tabulation, the seller can give up the cleaning machine or its operating supplies or environmental control equipment in order to sell any one or two of them. But the sale must not be allowed to take place if the system's cost-efficient operation cannot be insured by the seller's profit-improvement planning and customer information services.

"No Strategy"

The most dangerous attack against a system is the attempt to select out its PEIB components: the seller's *P*rescriptive *E*xpertise and *I*nformation *B*ase. This probe must be resisted at all costs. The seller's expertise and information resources are the brandable components of all systems. Often, they are the only brandable components. In the last analysis, they are the rockbottom leverage the seller has against desystemization. If they can be obtained separately, there may be little or no incentive left for the customer to acquire the total system. But the key reason for protecting expertise and information resources is that their premium values support the umbrella of premium price over the seller's entire system. Without them, a system will degenerate into a commodity.

The best defense against this type of desystemizing is to identify the seller's expertise and information firmly with the system as a whole. "After all," the seller may reason with a customer, "my prescriptive expertise is based on managing systems composed of my company's equipment and services. I know these components. I have confidence in them. I can predict their contribution to your improved profit. To ask me to apply my expertise to a system of foreign components deprives me of my quality control. It may defeat my ability and nullify my experience. It will certainly devalue my information base, which, as you know, has been painstakingly built up from experience with my own equipment and services in solving a wide range of problems. It may not be valid for other suppliers' systems. For these reasons, I must say *no*."

No seller likes to say "no" to a customer. Yet the desystemizing strategy of selecting only the seller's expertise and information base strikes so directly at the genesis of the systems concept that the seller has no choice. It must be rejected. The only way to avoid answering with a "no" response is to see that it isn't provoked in the first place. This is the seller's principal educational task.

The seller can always be certain of two facts about a system. For one, no matter how novel the hardware components may be initially, they will eventually become commodities. For this reason, the seller cannot allow customers to regard hardware as the core of their system. Second, the only component that can be branded against the inroads of commodity status is the "software" represented by the seller's prescriptive and applications expertise and information base. Every seller must educate customers to accept this basic truth from the very beginning. This is not easily reconciled when hardware is exclusive, innovative, technologically sophisticated, and personally exciting to the seller and even to customers. Nonetheless, it must be done. It is the seller's only strategy for avoiding the recurrent need to say "no" and to redirect customer attention to the seller's ongoing desire to say "yes" to customer profit improvement.

15

Preemption

A system's salability lies in its "customer advantage," which can be defined as the demand value added by improving customer profit. This customer advantage becomes the system advantage in the minds of customers, who evaluate systems both individually and competitively. Thus a system does more than *offer* a customer advantage; the system comes to *own* the advantage as its single most crucial selling point. This is preemption, a system's ability to seize an advantage uniquely to itself.

The preempted advantage of a system acts as its market-selecting mechanism. It selects customers in two ways. First, it seeks out and qualifies the segment of a market that has the greatest need for the system's advantage. Second, it comes to represent the system by acting as a shorthand way of describing its selective, or incremental, contribution. The customer advantage determines the market and documents the system's capabilities.

A system's customer advantage must conform to three requirements:

1. It must confer a truly superior added value over competitive systems as well as over the option of doing nothing about solving the customer's problem. It must make a positive contribution.

2. It must be at least equal to competitive systems in all important respects.
3. It must not be inferior to competitive systems in any important respect. It must be free from negative drawbacks.

The preemptive contribution of a system's customer advantage can be an attribute of the system and the way it is sold even though it may not be an attribute of any contributing element or component of the system itself. A superior customer advantage can be perceived by a market even in the absence of a single system component that is technically superior. The question of how much quality to build into a system therefore merits a minimal answer. Enough quality to deliver the customer advantage is enough quality.

A maximum quality system as determined by the aggregate quality load of its components may not be perceived as offering the maximum customer advantage. Minimal systems from the seller's perspective are often the preemptive systems from the customer's perspective.

The concept of preemption of customer advantage is not just an argument against overengineering, overpackaging, or overcosting, although it speaks powerfully against all three. It is essentially an argument in favor of the customer orientation of system prescription and application. And it provides the direction for establishing a system's branding: the capture of customer preference *because the customer's profit is being improved best,* not because the customer's system is constructed best.

In the final analysis, customer profit improvement, not an esoteric wizardry in assembling modular elements into packages or the alleged prestige of a consultant positioning, is what systems selling is all about.

Appendix 1

How Customers Plan and Evaluate the Lease Versus Buy Option for Systems

While many thousands of dollars may hinge on the choice between buying or leasing, the decision is made too frequently on the basis of insufficient information, sometimes with more reliance on intuition than on analysis. In this era of rising operating costs, the consequences of a wrong decision can be dramatic. Retailing is a typical example of the growth in leasing.

In recent years, more and more retailers have turned to leasing as a means of financing stores, warehouses, furniture, and fixtures. By acting as lessee, a retailer can acquire the use of assets immediately without having to raise funds equal to the purchase price. This is a particularly attractive attribute from the standpoint of financing expansion. The advantages of acting as lessor are also available to retailers. Today, for example, shopping centers are often owned by major retailers who lease space in the centers to other retailers. The owner-developer receives the benefit of any appreciation in the value of the center and thus is able to reduce his overall cost.

Adapted from "Leasing vs. Buying," originally published in *The Lybrand Journal,* Fall 1972, and reprinted by permission of Coopers & Lybrand. Content contributed by Dr. Jack Donis.

Ownership versus Short-Term Leasing

Ownership may be effected through outright purchase without indebtedness, through financed purchase, or, for all practical purposes, through a long-term lease. In an outright purchase, the buyer has full rights of ownership. Where the buyer obtains financing (before or after the purchase), his ownership is diminished by the limitations on his control of the asset. For example, in an installment purchase, the buyer's right to sell may be restricted by the lender's lien. In a long-term lease, the lessee lacks not only the right to sell but also all of the asset's residual rights except for any purchase options available.

Short-term leasing is an alternative to the above forms of ownership. Here, the lessee is freed of almost all the risks of ownership, including obsolescence and maintenance, but the amount of the rental naturally reflects these advantages. In choosing between some form of ownership (as described above) on the one hand and short-term leasing on the other, management is faced with such *operational* considerations as maintenance, risk of obsolescence, and the degree of control desired. If ownership is selected, a further decision—this one involving essentially *financial* considerations—is necessary with regard to the form of ownership. It is with this second, basically more complex, decision that this article is concerned. The focus will be specifically on the choice between outright purchase and long-term lease as a form of ownership.

Outright Purchase versus Long-Term Lease

The decision to buy or lease can be made only after a systematic evaluation of the relevant factors. The evaluation must be carried out in two stages: First, the advantages and disadvantages of purchase or lease must be considered, and, second, the cash flows under both alternatives must be compared.

Exhibit 1 * shows the principal advantages and disadvantages of leasing from both the lessor's and lessee's standpoint. This listing is only a guide. For both parties, the relative significance of the advantages and disadvantages depends on many factors. Major determinants are a company's size, financial position, and tax status. For example, to a heavily leveraged public company, the disadvantage of having to record additional debt may be considerable, even critical; the disadvantage may be insignificant to a privately held concern.

Analysis of Cash Flows

A cash flow analysis enables the potential lessee to contrast his cash position under both buying and leasing. This is essentially a capital budgeting procedure, and the method of developing and comparing cash flows should conform to the company's capital budgeting policies and practices. There are several comparison criteria in current use, among which the commonest are rate of return, discounted cash flow, and net cash position.

Outright purchase. The cash outflows in an outright purchase are the initial purchase price or, assuming the asset is purchased with borrowed funds, as is almost always the case, the subsequent principal and interest on the loan. There will also be operating expenses, such as maintenance and insurance, but these items are excluded from the comparison because they will be the same under both purchase and leasing assuming a net lease. The charge for depreciation is a noncash item. Cash inflows are the amount of the loan, the tax benefit from the yearly interest and depreciation, and the salvage value, if any.

Leasing. The lessee's cash flows are easier to define than the buyer's. The lessee pays a yearly rental, which is fully deductible. The lessee will thus have level annual outflows offset by the related tax benefit over the lease period. Salvage

---

* See the end of this appendix.

or residual value does not enter the picture because the lessee generally has no right of ownership in the asset. The table [on the following page] is a comparison of cash flows developed under both buying and leasing.

Comparing the cash flows. Once the annual cash flows from outright purchase and leasing have been developed, the next step is to contrast the flows by an accepted method (such as discounted cash flow) to determine which alternative gives the greater cash benefit or yield. In so doing, some consideration must be given to the effects of changes in the assumptions adopted. Examples could include a lengthening by the IRS of the depreciation period or a change in interest rates. In this manner, a series of contingencies could be introduced into the analysis, as follows: Assume a ten-year life and a borrowing at 10 percent. If outright purchase is better by X dollars, then

— A two-year increase in depreciable life reduces the benefit of outright purchase to $(X-Y)$ dollars.
— An upward change in interest rate reduces the benefit of outright purchase to $(X-Z)$ dollars.

Probabilities could be assigned to the contingencies, for example: that the depreciable life could be extended by two years, 30 percent; or that interest rates could rise by one-half a percentage point, 10 percent. Once the contingencies have been quantified, an overall probability of achieving the expected saving can then be calculated.

It must be stressed that the rate of return—the product of the cash-flow analysis—is not the exclusive or even, in some cases, the main determinant in deciding whether to buy or lease. Such factors as impact on financial statements, desire for operational flexibility, and loan restrictions, as well as other accounting, tax, economic, and financial considerations may be collectively at least as important. These aspects are essentially nonquantitative, but they can be evaluated with a satisfactory degree of accuracy by weighing the advantages and disadvantages.

Buying versus leasing; a comparison of cash flows ($100,000 asset).

Period	BUY Debt Service [a]	Principal Repayment	Interest Payment	Depreciation [b]	Interest Plus Depreciation	Tax Benefit at 50%	After-tax Cash Cost	Cumulative After-tax Cash Cost	LEASE Rental [c]	Tax Benefit at 50%	After-tax Cash Cost	Cumulative After-tax Cash Cost
1	$ 11,507	$ 3,614	$ 7,893	$ 12,500	$ 20,393	$10,197	$ 1,310	$ 1,310	$ 10,990	$ 5,495	$ 5,495	$ 5,495
2	11,507	3,912	7,595	11,667	19,262	9,631	1,876	3,186	10,990	5,495	5,495	10,990
3	11,507	4,234	7,273	10,833	18,106	9,053	2,454	5,640	10,990	5,495	5,595	16,485
4	11,507	4,583	6,924	10,000	16,924	8,462	3,045	8,685	10,990	5,495	5,495	21,980
5	11,507	4,961	6,546	9,167	15,713	7,856	3,651	12,336	10,990	5,495	5,495	27,475
6	11,507	5,370	6,137	8,333	14,470	7,235	4,272	16,608	10,990	5,495	5,495	32,970
7	11,507	5,813	5,694	7,500	13,194	6,597	4,910	21,518	10,990	5,495	5,495	38,465
8	11,507	6,292	5,215	6,667	11,882	5,941	5,566	27,084	10,990	5,495	5,495	43,960
9	11,507	6,810	4,697	5,833	10,530	5,265	5,242	33,326	10,990	5,495	5,495	49,455
10	11,507	7,372	4,135	5,000	9,135	4,567	6,940	40,266	10,990	5,495	5,495	54,950
11	11,507	7,979	3,528	4,167	7,695	3,848	7,659	47,925	10,990	5,495	5,495	60,445
12	11,507	8,637	2,870	3,333	6,203	3,101	8,406	56,331	10,990	5,495	5,495	65,940
13	11,507	9,349	2,158	2,500	4,658	2,329	9,178	65,509	10,990	5,495	5,495	71,435
14	11,507	10,120	1,387	1,667	3,054	1,527	9,980	75,489	10,990	5,495	5,495	76,930
15	11,507	10,954	553	833	1,386	693 [d]	10,814	86,303	10,990	5,495	5,495	82,425
	$172,605	$100,000	$72,605	$100,000	$172,605	$86,302 [d]	$86,303		$164,850	$82,425	$82,425 [e]	

Notes

(a) $100,000 of debt borrowed at 8%. The debt service, payable quarterly in arrears, will be sufficient to amortize the loan fully over 15 years. (b) Asset cost of $100,000 will be depreciated over 15 years using the sum-of-the-years digits method. It was assumed that the asset had no salvage value. (c) Rental on a 15-year lease will be payable quarterly in arrears. The rental was based on an interest factor of 7¼%. It was assumed that the lessee's credit would require 8% interest. Since the lessor retains the depreciation ben-

efits of the asset, he can charge a rent based on 7¼% even though he has financed the acquisition at 8%. (d) Present worth of $86,302 cost of buying, at 8%, is $41,198. (e) Present worth of $82,425 cost of leasing, at 8%, is $47,034.

COMMENT ON NOTES d and e: When comparing the cumulative after-tax cash costs, buying is the more expensive alternative by about $4,000. However, present-valuing the annual outflows results in buying's being the more economical alternative by approximately $6,000.

Accounting Treatment

Accounting for leases is the subject of two opinions of the Accounting Principles Board (APB) of the American Institute of CPAs: Opinion Number 5 (relating to lessees), issued in 1964, and Opinion Number 7 (relating to lessors), issued in 1966.

Lessees. According to APB 5, "The central question is whether assets and liabilities are created by leases which convey the rights to use property if no equity is accumulated in the property by the lessee." The Board distinguished two examples at opposite extremes, the conventional lease that exchanges the right to use property for rent, and the lease essentially equivalent to an installment purchase. The Board considered that the first type does not create equity for the lessee. "The rights and obligations under leases which convey merely the right to use property, without an equity in the property accruing to the lessee, fall into the category of pertinent information which should be disclosed in schedules or notes rather than by recording assets and liabilities in the financial statements." With regard to the second type of lease arrangement, the Opinion declares, "Some lease agreements are essentially equivalent to installment purchases of property. . . . The property and related obligation should be included as an asset and liability in the balance sheet if the terms of the lease result in the creation of a material equity in the property."

Determining lessee equity. In Paragraphs 10 and 11, APB Opinion 5 sets forth guidelines for determining whether the lessee has equity in the property: "It is unlikely that such equity can be created under a lease which either party may cancel unilaterally for reasons other than the occurrence of some remote contingency." The Opinion goes on to enumerate a series of conditions considered to create a presumption that a noncancellable lease is a purchase:

— The initial lease term is materially shorter than the property's useful life, and the lessee has the right to renew for the balance of the useful life, or has purchase options, at bargain prices.

— The lessor acquires the property to meet the lessee's special needs, and the property is in all probability useless to any other lessee or for any other purpose.
— The lessee assumes all the incidents of ownership, such as taxes, insurance, and maintenance.
— The lessee guarantees the lessor's obligations with respect to the property leased.
— The lessee treats the property as a purchase for tax purposes.

If the facts indicate that the lease is in substance a purchase, it should be capitalized by appropriately discounting the aggregate future lease rental payments. If the lease is deemed to be a noncapitalizable lease, it should be disclosed in a footnote to the financial statements. This footnote should be sufficient for the reader "to assess the effects of lease commitments upon the financial position and results of operations, both present and prospective, of the lessee" (see APB Opinion No. 5).

In practice, many accountants use the following rule of thumb in determining the buildup of material equity. If all the purchase options and the present value of the future renewal options at the beginning of the applicable renewal periods exceed the undepreciated book balance of the assets at the respective option or renewal dates, a material equity has not been created and capitalization is not required. Of course, the very concept of rule of thumb implies general rather than absolute applicability. The accountant may properly set aside the "rule" where circumstances warrant it.

Lessors. APB Opinion Number 7 defines two alternative methods for lessors—financing and operating. The financing method should be used by companies acting as lessors primarily as a result of being in the business of lending money. Banks and insurance companies belong in this category. Institutions entering into such leases generally pass the risks and most of the rewards of ownership on to the lessee, and the lessors are satisfied to recover their investment along with an adequate return. The lessor's income is similar to interest income, defined by Opinion 7 as the excess of aggregate rentals over the cost (less residual value at the termination of the lease) of the leased property. This excess is taken into income in the same way as interest might be reported on a comparable loan.

The operating method, on the other hand, should be used by lessors retaining the incidents of ownership; examples would include building owners and short-term car-rental companies. The income reported is the amount of rent due under the lease.

Thus, in the APB's view, the accounting treatment of the lessor depends upon his business, his objectives in entering into the lease, and the risks and rewards of ownership retained. Two other provisions of APB 7 should be noted because of their potential effect on financial statements. Under Paragraph 11, the lessor is allowed to expense "initial costs"—i.e., costs of negotiating and closing the lease—as incurred and to recognize as revenue in the same period, in addition to normal revenue, a portion of the unearned revenue equal to the initial costs. Under Paragraph 12 and Interpretation No. 1 of the Opinion, manufacturers who lease their product as a marketing method are allowed—subject to certain specified conditions—to record in the year the lease is contracted the same manufacturing revenues, costs, and profits as would have been reported had the product been sold outright. (Here, of course, the profit would be recognized for financial reporting purposes in the year of the lease, whereas the cash proceeds would be realized over an extended period.)

Conflicting points. A major objection to the two Opinions arises from the presence of certain inconsistencies. For example, grant that a lease conforms to the criteria for reporting under the financing method, as defined in Opinion 7. Does the lease then have to be capitalized on the books of the lessee? (The Board discussed this question in Opinion 7, stating that the decision as to treatment by the lessee should be made independently of the lessor's treatment and vice versa.) However, the Board (or its successor, the Financial Accounting Standards Board) is considering these inconsistencies, as well as other problems connected with the reporting of leases, and it expects to issue a new opinion or further interpretations.

Tax Considerations

There are two ways in which a lease can be treated for tax purposes, as a true lease or as a form of financing. If the lease is viewed as a true lease, the lessee is entitled to a deduction, in the appropriate period, for his annual rental expenses. (Normally, the appropriate period is the period in which the liability for rent is incurred, in accordance with the terms of the lease, granted that the timing of the liability is not unreasonable.) If the lease is viewed as a form of financing, the lessee is deemed the property's equitable owner, and is thus permitted to deduct the depreciation and interest expense.

The test the IRS applies to determine whether a lease is a true lease or a form of financing is basically an evaluation of the purchase options. If the lessee can purchase the property for less than the fair market value or for an amount approximately equal to what the debt balance would have been had the asset been bought outright, the transaction is viewed as a financing arrangement. If the lessee has a purchase option in an amount substantially exceeding the probable fair market value or the debt balance, the transaction would probably be recognized as a lease.

Treatment of sale and leaseback. An asset sold in a sale-and-leaseback arrangement may qualify as a "Section 1231 asset," that is, a depreciable asset on land used in the taxpayer's trade or business. The Internal Revenue Code provides that net gain on the sale of Section 1231 assets, to the extent that they are not subject to depreciation recapture, should be treated as a capital gain, whereas net loss may be deducted from income as an ordinary loss. This treatment allows the future lessee great flexibility in timing a sale and leaseback to best fit his tax posture. For example, in a high-bracket year, a company could sell and lease back an asset that has a market value substantially below book and obtain a large ordinary deduction. The danger here is that the IRS could declare the transaction a sham and disallow the deduction.

Typically, the Service has contended that a sale has not really taken place, but that the would-be-seller has retained control over the asset while merely obtaining financing with the asset as collateral. The IRS position has been strongest where the sale and lease were not for fair market value and the period of the lease was lengthy. Accordingly, the taxpayer's strongest defense has been in his ability to show that the negotiations were at arm's length, the terms called for fair market value, the buyer-lessor was not a related party, and the basic lease term was under 30 years. These defenses cannot be overemphasized. Case law has gone both ways, but the taxpayer has generally been successful where he has been able to prove that the sale price and the rental were at no less than fair market value.

The Business Relationship

A final aspect of the lease-buy decision relates to the lessor-lessee relationship. If the lessor encounters financial difficulties, under certain circumstances the prospective lessee can be adversely affected. That is, depending upon the terms of the lease and the lessor's financing arrangements, a lender might look to the property to satisfy a default by the lessor. Although careful wording of the agreement can afford a measure of protection, it is essential that the lessee look into the prospective lessor's financial condition, business reputation, and client relationships. If the findings are favorable, negotiations may be carried out with a minimum of delay and expense. If the findings are unfavorable, the prospective lessee might still wish to proceed, relying on the protective clauses in the agreement, or he might abandon the lease (at least with that party) entirely.

The lessee should examine the lessor's purposes in entering into the lease to determine how they mesh with his own. (The foregoing analysis of the advantages and disadvantages of leasing has been oriented towards both parties.) There is no reason why the examination cannot be mutual. If both parties have an understanding of the other's goals, the chances of a mutually satisfactory lease would be enhanced.

The Overall Perspective

Many of the varied facets of leasing pertinent to buy-or-lease decisions are undergoing change. The APB is currently reviewing, and the FASB will also consider, the treatment of leases by both lessees and lessors, the courts in tax cases are deliberating over the recognition of gain and loss on sale and leaseback, and the financial community is becoming more and more sophisticated in evaluating lease commitments and determining return on investment. Therefore, anyone weighing the pros and cons of leasing must be sure that all the assumptions on which the analysis is based are *currently* valid. Finally, it cannot be overstressed that the decision to buy or lease is a very complex one, and requires a comprehensive assessment of both objective and subjective factors before an economically correct decision can be made.

Exhibit 1. Leasing advantages and disadvantages.

Lessee Advantages

One hundred percent financing of the cost of the property (the lease is based on the full cost), on terms that may be individually tailored to the lessee.

Possible avoidance of existing loan indenture restrictions on new debt financing. Free of these restrictions, the lessee may be able to increase his base, as lease obligations are generally not reflected on the balance sheet, although the lease obligation will probably require footnote disclosure in the financial statements. (It should be noted, however, that a number of the more recent loan indentures restrict lease commitments.)

General allowability of rental deductions for the term of the lease, without problems or disputes about the property's depreciable life.

Possibly higher net book income during the earlier years of the basic lease term than under outright ownership. Rental payments in the lease's earlier years are generally lower than the combined interest expense and depreciation (even on the straight-line method) that a corporate property owner would otherwise have charged in the income statement.

Potential reduction in state and city franchise and income taxes, since the property factor, which is generally one of the three factors in the allocation formula, is reduced.

Full deductibility of rent payment, notwithstanding the fact that the rent is partially based on the cost of the land.

(continued)

Lessee Disadvantages

Loss of residual rights to the property upon the lease's termination. When the lessee has full residual rights, the transaction cannot be a true lease; instead, it is a form of financing. In a true lease, the lessee may have the right to purchase or renew, but the exercise of these options requires payments to the lessor after the full cost of the property has been amortized.

Rentals greater than comparable debt service. Since the lessor generally borrows funds with which to buy the asset to be leased, the rent is based on the lessor's debt service plus a profit factor. This amount may exceed the debt service that the lessee would have had to pay had he purchased the property.

Loss of operating and financing flexibility. If an asset were owned outright and a new, improved model became available, the owner could sell or exchange the old model for the new one. This may not be possible under a lease. Moreover, if interest rates decreased, the lessee would have to continue paying at the old rate, whereas the owner of the asset could refinance his debt at a lower rate.

Loss of tax benefits from accelerated depreciation and high interest deductions in early years. These benefits would produce a temporary cash saving if the property had been purchased instead of leased.

Lessor Advantages

Higher rate of return than on investment in straight debt. To compensate for risk and lack of marketability, the lessor can charge the lessee a higher effective rate—particularly after considering the lessor's tax benefits—than the lessor could obtain by lending the cost of the property at the market rate.

The lessor has the leased asset as security. Should the lessee have financial trouble, the lessor can reclaim a specific asset instead of having to take his place with the general creditors.

Retention of the property's residual value upon the lease's termination. The asset's cost is amortized over the basic lease term. If, upon the lease's expiration, the lessee abandons the property, the lessor can sell it. If the lessee renews or purchases, the proceeds to the lessor would represent substantially all profit.

Lessor Disadvantages

Dependence upon lessee's ability to maintain payments on a timely basis.

Vulnerability to unpredictable changes in the tax law that (a) reduce tax benefits and related cash flow, or (b) significantly extend depreciable life. The latter measure would lessen the projected return upon which the lessor based his investment.

Probable negative after-tax cash flow in later years. As the lease progresses, an increasing percentage of the rent goes towards nondeductible amortization of the principal. The interest and depreciation deductions (under the accelerated method) both decline as the lease progresses.

Potentially large tax on disposition of asset imposed by the Internal Revenue Code's depreciation recapture provisions.

Appendix 2
Model System Lease

LEASE NO. _____

LESSOR _____(herein called "Lessor")

LESSEE _____(herein called "Lessee")

ADDRESS _____

1. LEASE
Lessor hereby leases to Lessee, and Lessee hereby leases from Lessor, the following personal property (herein called "system"):

PLACE OF INSTALLATION

Street	City	State

2. TERM AND RENT
The term of this lease shall commence at the time of execution and acceptance of this Agreement by Lessor, or upon delivery of the system to Lessee, whichever occurs first, and shall continue for a period of _____ months. As rent for the system throughout the term hereof, Lessee hereby agrees to pay Lessor the sum of $_____ per month beginning _____ 19____, and the same amount on the same day of each consecutive month thereafter for the term hereof, first and last _____ payments in the amount of $_____ being payable at the time of signing this Agreement. The payments provided for herein shall be payable at the above office of Lessor in _____ or at any place otherwise designated by Lessor.

147

3. TAXES; INDEMNITY

Lessee agrees to comply with all laws, regulations, and orders relating to this lease and to pay all license fees, assessments, and sales, use, property, excise, and other taxes now or hereafter imposed by any government body or agency upon any Equipment, or the use thereof or the rentals hereunder (other than taxes on or measured by the net income of Lessor), and to assume the risk of liability arising from or pertaining to the possession, operation, or use of such Equipment or the return of such Equipment to Lessor. Lessee does hereby agree to indemnify, hold safe and harmless from and against the covenants to defend Lessor, its servants and agents, against any and all claims, costs, expenses, damages, and liabilities, arising from or pertaining to the use, possession, or operation of such Equipment. Any fees, taxes, or other lawful charges paid by Lessor upon failure of Lessee to make such payments, shall at Lessor's option become immediately due from Lessee to Lessor. The indemnities contained in this Paragraph shall survive the termination of this Agreement.

4. IDENTIFICATION; PERSONAL PROPERTY

No right, title, or interest in the system shall pass to Lessee other than, conditioned upon Lessee's compliance with and fulfillment of the terms and conditions of this Agreement, the right to maintain possession and use the system for the full lease term. At its option, Lessor may require plates or markings to be affixed to or placed on the Equipment indicating Lessor is the owner. Lessor and Lessee both hereby confirm their intent that the system shall always remain and be deemed personal property even though said Equipment may hereafter become attached or affixed to realty. Lessee agrees to take such action, at its own expense, as may be necessary to prevent any third party from acquiring any interest in said Equipment by virtue of said Equipment being deemed to be a part of realty.

5. WARRANTIES

All warranties made by the manufacturers of the Equipment to the extent assignable, hereby are assigned by Lessor in their entirety to the Lessee.

6. USE; ASSIGNMENT

Lessee will cause the system to be operated in accordance with any applicable manufacturer's manuals or instructions, by competent and duly qualified personnel only, in accordance with applicable government regulations, if any, and for business purposes only. Lessee agrees not to sell, assign, sublet, pledge, hypothecate, or otherwise encumber or suffer a lien upon or against any interest in this Agreement or the system or to remove the Equipment from its place of installation without Lessor's prior consent.

7. DEFAULT

To the extent permitted by applicable law, Lessee will pay on demand, as a late charge, an amount equal to 10% of each installment of rent in the event such installment or any part thereof remains overdue for more than 10 days. If (i) Lessee shall fail to make any rent payment promptly when due, or (ii) Lessee shall fail to perform or observe any other covenant, condition, or agreement hereunder, or (iii) any representation or warranty made by Lessee herein or in any document furnished Lessor in connection herewith shall prove to be incorrect at any time, or (iv) Lessee shall become insolvent or bankrupt or make an assignment for the benefit of creditors or consent to the appointment of a trustee or receiver, or a trustee or a receiver shall be appointed for Lessee or for a substantial part of its property, or bankruptcy, reorganization, or insolvency proceedings shall be instituted by or against Lessee, then, upon the occurrence of any such event, Lessor may at its option declare this Agreement to be in default and may do one or more of the following with respect to any or all Equipment as Lessor in its sole discretion shall elect, to the extent permitted by, and subject to compliance with any mandatory requirements of, applicable law then in effect: (a) cause Lessee to (and Lessee agrees that it will), upon written demand of Lessor and at Lessee's expense, promptly return any or all Equipment to Lessor in accordance with all of the terms of Paragraph 11 hereof, or Lessor, at its option, may enter upon the premises where such Equipment is located and take immediate possession of and remove the same, all without liability to Lessor for damage to property or otherwise; (b) sell any or all of the Equipment at public or private sale, with or without notice to Lessee or advertisement, or otherwise dispose of, hold, use, operate, lease to others, or keep idle such Equipment, all as Lessor in its sole discretion may determine and all free and clear of any rights of Lessee and without any duty to account to Lessee for such action or inaction or for any proceeds with respect thereto; (c) by written notice to Lessee, cause Lessee to (and Lessee agrees that it will) pay to Lessor (as liquidated damages for loss of a bargain and not as a penalty) on the date specified in such notice an amount (plus interest thereon at the rate of 10% per annum from said date to the date of actual payment) equal to all unpaid rent payments which absent a default would have been payable hereunder for the full term thereof; and/or (d) Lessor may exercise any other right or remedy which may be available to it under the Uniform Commercial Code or any other applicable law or proceed by appropriate court action to enforce the terms hereof or to recover damages for the breach hereof or to rescind this Agreement as to any or all Equipment. In addition, Lessee shall continue to be liable for all indemnities under this Agreement and for all legal fees and other costs and expenses resulting from the foregoing defaults or the exercise of Lessor's remedies, including placing any equipment in the condition required by Paragraph 11 hereof. No remedy referred to in this Paragraph is intended to be exclusive, but each shall be cumulative and in addition to any other remedy referred to above or otherwise available to Lessor at law or in equity. No express or implied waiver by Lessor of any default shall constitute a waiver of any other default by Lessee or a waiver of any of Lessor's rights. To the extent permitted by applicable law, Lessee hereby waives any rights now or hereafter conferred by statute or otherwise which may require Lessor to sell, lease, or otherwise use any Equipment in mitigation of Lessor's damages as set forth in this Paragraph or which may otherwise limit or modify any of Lessor's rights or remedies under this Paragraph.

8. NOTICES

For the purpose of this Agreement, any notices and demands required to be given shall be given to the parties in writing and by regular mail at the address herein set forth, or to such other address as the parties may hereafter substitute by written notice.

9. REPAIRS; LOSS AND DAMAGE

Lessee, at its own cost and expense, shall keep all Equipment in good repair, condition, and working order, in accordance with any applicable manufacturer's manuals or instructions, and shall furnish all parts, mechanisms, devices, and servicing required therefor. All such parts, mechanisms, and devices shall immediately become the property of Lessor and part of the Equipment for all purposes hereof. In the event that any item of Equipment shall become lost, stolen, destroyed, damaged beyond repair, or rendered permanently unfit for use for any reason, or in the event of any condemnation, confiscation, theft, or seizure or requisition of title to or use of such item, Lessee shall promptly pay to Lessor an amount equal to the aggregate unpaid rent payments for the full term of the lease of such item, whereupon such items shall become the property of Lessee and Lessor will transfer to Lessee, without recourse or warranty, all of Lessor's right, title, and interest, if any, therein.

10. INSURANCE
Lessee shall maintain on the system, at its own expense, property damage and liability insurance in such amounts, against such risks, in such form and with such insurers as shall be satisfactory to Lessor, provided, however, that the amount of property damage insurance shall not be less than the greater of the full replacement value of the Equipment or the installments of rent then remaining unpaid hereunder. Each insurance policy will name Lessee as an insured and Lessor as an additional insured, and shall contain a clause requiring the insurer to give to Lessor at least 10 days' prior written notice of any alteration in the terms of such policy or of the cancellation thereof. At Lessor's option, Lessee shall furnish to Lessor a certificate of insurance carrier or other evidence satisfactory to Lessor that such insurance coverage is in effect provided, however, that Lessor shall be under no duty either to ascertain the existence of or to examine such insurance or to advise Lessee in the event such insurance shall not comply with the requirements hereof.

11. RETURN OF EQUIPMENT
Upon expiration of the lease, Lessee, at its own expense, will immediately return all Equipment in the same condition as when delivered to Lessee, ordinary wear and tear excepted, to Lessor at such location as Lessor shall designate.

12. FURTHER ASSURANCES
Lessee will promptly execute and deliver to Lessor such further documents and take such further action as Lessor may request in order to more effectively carry out the intent and purpose hereof, including, without limitation, (i) the filing of a financial or continuation statement with respect hereto, in accordance with the laws of any applicable jurisdictions and (ii) the taking of such further action as Lessor may deem desirable to fully protect Lessor's interest hereunder in accordance with the Uniform Commercial Code or other applicable law. Lessee hereby authorizes Lessor to effect any such filing as aforesaid (including the filing of any such financing statements without the signature of Lessee), and, at the option of Lessor. Lessor's costs and expenses with respect thereto shall constitute additional rent, payable on demand.

13. NON-CANCELLABLE LEASE
This Agreement cannot be cancelled or terminated except as expressly provided herein.

14. LESSEE'S OBLIGATIONS UNCONDITIONAL
Lessee hereby agrees that Lessee's obligation to pay all rent and any other amounts owing hereunder shall be absolute and unconditional under all circumstances, including, without limitation, the following circumstances: (i) any set off, counterclaim, recoupment, defense, or other right which Lessee may have against Lessor, any seller or manufacturer of any Equipment, or anyone else for any reason whatsoever; (ii) the existence of any liens, encumbrances, or rights of others whatsoever with respect to any Equipment, whether or not resulting from claims against Lessor not related to the ownership of such Equipment; or (iii) any other event or circumstances whatsoever, whether or not similar to any of the foregoing. If for any reason whatsoever this Agreement shall be terminated in whole or in part by operation of law or otherwise except as specifically provided herein or shall be disaffirmed by any trustee or receiver

for Lessee or Lessor, Lessee nonetheless agrees to pay to Lessor an amount equal to each rent payment at the time such payment would have become due and payable in accordance with the terms hereof had this Agreement not been terminated or disaffirmed in whole or in part. Each rent or other payment made by Lessee hereunder shall be final and Lessee will not seek to recover all or any part of such payment from Lessor for any reason whatsoever.

15. MISCELLANEOUS

Any provision of this Agreement which is unenforceable in any jurisdiction shall, as to such jurisdiction, be ineffective to the extent of such unenforceability without invalidating the remaining provisions hereof, and any such unenforceability in any jurisdiction shall not render unenforceable such provisions in any other jurisdiction. To the extent permitted by applicable law Lessee hereby waives any provision of law which renders any provision hereof unenforceable in any respect. Any waiver of the terms hereof shall be effective only in the specific instance and for the specific purpose given. Time is of the essence in this Agreement. The captions in this Agreement are for convenience only and shall not define or limit any of the terms hereof. This Agreement shall in all respects be governed by and construed in accordance with the laws of this state, including all matters of construction, validity, and performance.

This agreement consists of the foregoing. No agreements or understanding shall be binding on either of the parties hereto unless specifically set forth in this Agreement. The term "Lessee" as used herein shall mean and include any and all Lessees who sign hereunder, each of whom shall be jointly and severally bound thereby.

Executed this ___ day of _____, 19___

_____
Witness

By execution hereof, the signer hereby certifies that he has read this Agreement, and that he is duly authorized to execute this lease on behalf of Lessee.

LESSEE:

By _____
Authorized Signature and Title

LESSOR:

By _____
Authorized Signature and Title

Appendix 3

How Customers Plan and Evaluate Capital Expenditures for Systems

---

The capital budgeting process contains four steps: (1) project planning, (2) evaluation and decision making, (3) control and audit of cash commitments, (4) post-audit evaluating and reporting of results.

The first step in capital budgeting proceeds on the assumption that a company has a formal long-range plan or, at the least, the proposed project fits into the mainstream of the corporation's interest. Implicit in a proposal is a forecast of markets, revenues, costs, expenses, profit. These aspects of capital budgeting are the most important, most time-consuming, most critical phase, and largely outside of the area of expertise of the financial executive. A major project generally affects marketing, engineering, manufacturing, and finance.

The uncertainties surrounding a long-range forecast are often great enough to throw doubt on the effectiveness of the entire decision-making process. Probability analysis of

Adapted from "The Capital Budgeting Process," originally published as a monograph by Coopers & Lybrand, 1973, and reprinted by permission. Content contributed by Dr. Jack Donis.

success/failure becomes important in view of the uncertainties. A relatively simple approach to evaluating uncertainty is discussed later. However, sophisticated probability analysis and computer simulation can be beneficial in giving credulity to major long-range projections in the face of great uncertainty. Unless this phase of capital budgeting is made reliable and meaningful, the decision-making phase simply becomes an exercise in arithmetic.

The second stage, project evaluation and decision-making methods, has received major attention in accounting and financial publications. There is general agreement that the time-adjusted cash flow methods (net present value and discounted cash flow [DCF] rate of return) are most meaningful guides to the investment decision; however, there is still place for cash payback analysis in appraising the financial risks inherent in a projection. These methods will be examined and brought into perspective for use in the proposed model. Within certain limits, and they can be identified, these measures will give the best tools for appraising proposals. They do not produce the magic go, no-go answer. They give management guidance. No matter what quantitative guidelines are developed, qualitative factors will be important in the final decision—the personal judgments and preferences of the project sponsor and management cannot be discounted.

The third step, control and audit of cash, is the simplest step in the budgeting process once the source of funds has been determined and committed. After approval, the project should be treated as any other budgeted item, with payment schedules determined and variances reported and explained. Major overspending can impair the validity of the investment decision, and even invalidate the entire process.

A caution is appropriate at this point. When a proposal calls for a specific investment it is implicit that no more than that amount will be spent. Overspending of any significant amount cannot be permitted. Similarly, a project sponsor should not come back the next year for additional funds because he underestimated his original request. When either of these events occurs, it becomes necessary to refigure the entire project on the total cash outlay. Unfortunately, at this point the firm is already irrevocably committed to the project and the new calculations are after the fact.

The fourth step, post-audit evaluating and reporting of results of investment, is a concept that everyone agrees needs doing, but is rarely done. As will be reviewed below, capital investments are projected on an incremental basis, on a cash basis, and on an internal rate of return basis over the life of the investment. Regular financial records and reports are on an annual basis, an accrual basis, or on a rate of return by individual years. A major problem is that many projects become an integral part of a larger, existing investment and the new project cannot be separated from the existing one. The post audit of the incremental segment may become obscure or meaningless. As a result, many incremental investments cannot be appraised against objectives, for example, a large rate of return. The large projected incremental rate of return may become diluted when merged with a larger investment. There may be general disappointment because the new investment results have not lived up to forecasts and, yet, the projected earnings and cash flow of the incremental investment may be right on target. New criteria for post audit may have to be determined to affect post audit for many projects at the time the original projections are made so that management knows how it will measure results against plan. One criterion may be cash flow. Another criterion may be the development of pro forma statements comparing financial income before and after the additional investment, that is, a financial model. The main point is that good budgeting calls for comparisons of projections and results, and though the project evaluation criteria may not be susceptible to audit in many cases, it should not preclude the establishment of other criteria for post-audit purposes at the time the original projection is made. The use of pro forma statements indicating total results as well as impact on earnings per share before and after the investment may be the appropriate basis for appraisal of the additional investment.

Principles of Capital Investment Analysis

This section describes the specific concepts used to evaluate major capital expenditure projects and programs within the scope of the capital budgeting process. The underlying concepts and methods used are examined to bring into focus the economic consequences of a capital expenditure.

When a capital expenditure is proposed, the project must be evaluated and the economic consequences of the commitment of funds determined before referring it to a budget committee for review or to management for approval. How are the economic consequences described best? This is done in two steps:

First, set up the project into a standard economic model that can be used for all projects no matter how dissimilar they may be.

$$\text{Benefits} - \text{Cost} = \text{Cash Flow}$$

To describe the formula in accounting terminology:

Benefits: Projected cash revenue from sales and other sources

Costs: Nonrecurring cash outlays for assets, plus recurring operating expenses

Cash Flow: Net income after taxes plus non-cash charges for such items as depreciation

Thus, if the model were stated in a conventional accounting form it would appear as:

Add: Cash revenues projected (Benefits)
Less: Cash investment outlay and cash expenses (Costs)
Total: Cash flow

The "benefits less costs" model is usually developed within the framework of the firm's chart of accounts and supported with prescribed supplementary schedules that show the basis of the projection.

It should be apparent that in setting up an economic model, the conventional accrual accounting concept, net income after taxes, has been abandoned. The established criterion is cash flow—net income after tax plus non-cash charges.

Second, adjust the cash flow into relevant financial terms. The cash flow projected for each year over the life of the proposal has to be translated into financial terms that are valid; that is, translate the annual dollar cash flows to a common dollar value in a base year. This concept must not be confused with attempts to adjust for changes in the purchasing power of the dollar.

The calculations assume no significant erosion in the purchasing power of the dollar. Should this occur the time-adjusted common dollar concept may require adjustments for the diminished real value (purchasing power) of future dollar payments. The common dollar value concept used in capital budgeting adjusts for time value only. This is achieved through the development of the concept of discounting and present value that will be examined in the next section. An examination of how a simple two-step model is developed will illustrate the rationale of this approach.

In the first step we set up the economic model: benefits minus costs equals cash flow. To complete this model we need to identify in detail all economic benefits and costs associated with the project. Benefits typically take the form of sales revenues and other income. Costs include nonrecurring outlays for fixed assets, investments in working capital, and recurring outlays for payrolls, materials, expenses, etc.

For each element of benefits and costs that the project involves we forecast the amount of change for each year. How far ahead do we forecast? For as long as the expenditure decision will continue to have effects; that is, for as long as they generate costs and significant benefits. Forecasts are made for each year of the project's life; we call the year of decision "Year Zero," the next year "Year One," and so on. When the decision's effects extend so far into the future that estimates are very conjectural the model stops forecasting at a "planning horizon" (10 to 15 years), far enough in the future to establish clearly whether the basis for the decision is a correct one.

We apply a single economic concept in forecasting costs: opportunity cost. The opportunity cost of a resource (asset) is what the company loses from not using it in an alternative use or exchanging it for another asset. For example, if cash has earning power of 15 percent after taxes we speak of the cash as having an opportunity cost of 15 percent. Whenever an asset is acquired for a cash payment, the opportunity cost is, of course, the cash given up to acquire it. It is harder to establish the opportunity cost of committing assets already owned or controlled. If owned land committed to a project would otherwise be sold, the opportunity cost is the after-tax proceeds from the sale. The opportunity cost of using productive equipment, transportation vehicles, or plant facilities is the incremental profit lost because these resources are unavailable for other purposes. If the alternative to using owned facilities is idleness, the opportunity cost is zero. Although opportunity costs are difficult to identify and measure, they must be considered if we are to describe the economic consequences of a decision as accurately as possible. An understanding of this concept of opportunity cost is probably the most critical to this economic analysis and is generally quite foreign to the businessman.

At the end of the first step we have an economic model for the project's life showing forecast cash flows for each year. In the second step we convert the results into financial terms that are meaningful for decision making. We must take into account the one measurable financial effect of an investment decision left out in step 1: time. Dollars shown in different years of the model cannot be compared since time makes them of dissimilar value. We clearly recognize that if we have an opportunity to invest funds and earn 15 percent a year and we have a choice of receiving $1,000 today or a year from now we will take the $1,000 today, so that it can be invested and earn $150. On this basis $1,000 available a year from now is worth less than $1,000 today. It is this adjustment for time that is required to make cash flows in different years comparable; that is, discounting.

This time value of funds available for investment is known

as the opportunity cost of capital. This should not be confused with the cost of raising capital—debt or equity, or with the company's average earnings rate. Like the opportunity cost of any resource, the opportunity cost of capital is what it will cost the company to use capital for an investment project in terms of what this capital could earn elsewhere.

The opportunity cost of capital is alternatively referred to as the minimum acceptable rate of interest, the marginal rate of interest, the minimum rate of return, the marginal rate of return, and the cost of capital. Whatever the term used, and they are used loosely and interchangeably, it reflects the rate the corporation decides it can be reasonably sure of getting by using the money in another way. It is developed through the joint efforts of management, who identifies relevant opportunities, and the controller, who translates management's judgment into a marginal rate.

Another simple economic concept must be introduced: incremental cost, sometimes called differential cost or marginal cost. By definition it is the change in cost (or revenue) that results from a decision to expand or contract an operation. It is the difference in total cost. In performing the capital budgeting analysis we deal with incremental costs (revenues) only. Sunk or existing costs are not relevant to the evaluation and decision.

Throughout this study all references to costs and revenues are on an incremental basis.

Rationale of Discounting and Present Value

Discounting is a technique used to find the value today or "present value" of money paid or received in the future. This value is found from the following formula:

Future Dollar Amount × Discount Factor = Present Value

The discount factor depends on the opportunity cost of capital expressed as an interest rate and a time period. Table 1 illustrates how discount factors are usually displayed. The discount factors are grouped according to the annual interest rate, expressed as the present value of $1.00, and then listed according to the year the amount comes due. The table should be read this way: When a dollar earns 10 percent per year uniformly over time, a dollar received at the end of the second year is equivalent to (worth) about 86 cents today.

Table 1. Present value of $1.00 at 10 percent.

YEAR	PRESENT VALUE (TODAY'S VALUE)
0–1	$0.9516
1–2	0.8611
2–3	0.7791
3–4	0.7050
4–5	0.6379

Arithmetic and Concept of Present Value

To adjust the model's results for the time element we "discount" both the positive and negative cash flow forecasts for each period at the company's marginal rate of return to determine their present value. This discounting process makes the forecasts equivalent in time. We can now add the present values of these cash flow forecasts to derive the net present value (NPV). The NPV is a meaningful measure of the economic consequences of an investment decision since it measures all benefits and all costs, including the opportunity cost of capital.

When the net present value of a proposed investment is determined we are ready to decide whether it should be accepted. This is done by comparing it to the economic consequences of doing nothing or of accepting an alternative. The general rule followed in comparing alternative projects is to choose the course of action that results in the highest net present value.

Table 2 illustrates the cash flow forecasts and time-value

calculations for a typical proposal to invest in a new project when the alternative is to do nothing; that is, maintain liquidity rather than invest. A discount rate of 10 percent is assumed as the company's marginal rate.

Table 2. Arithmetic of determining net present value.

YEAR	BENEFITS	COSTS	CASH FLOW	PV OF $1 @ 10%	DISCOUNTED CASH FLOW
0	$ 0	$(500)	$(500)	1.000	$(500)
0–1	425	(200)	225	.952	214
1–2	425	(200)	225	.861	194
2–3	350	(200)	150	.779	117
3–4	250	(200)	50	.705	35
Total	$1,450	$(1,300)	$150		$60 NPV

The proposed project will cost $500 in year 0, and cash operating expenses thereafter will be $200 per year for four years. Assume the cash benefits will be positive but decline over the four years and total $1,450. The cash flow is negative in the year of investment but positive in the succeeding years and there is a net positive cash flow over the life of the project of $150 before discounting. When the cash flow forecasts are made equivalent in time by multiplying each annual cash flow by the present value of the dollar for each period, the time-adjusted cash flow is determined, and the net present value is found to be $60. The proposed investment is better than doing nothing since all costs are covered, the 10 percent opportunity cost of the corporation's funds is realized, and in addition, the project will yield an additional $60 return.

Table 2 indicates an NPV of $60. Depending on the cash flow and/or the discount rate, the NPV could be negative or zero. If the NPV were zero, the company would have projected earnings exactly equal to its marginal rate of 10 percent. If there were no alternative projects, and the only alternative were to do nothing, the project with the NPV of zero would be accepted since the company would earn its marginal rate of return. (As explained later, the NPV of zero would yield the discounted cash flow rate of return; that is, 10 percent.) If the NPV were negative because of an inadequate cash flow, assuming the same 10 percent marginal rate required by management, it would mean the project would earn less than 10 percent, and it would be rejected.

There are a number of evaluation methods that are employed in capital budgeting; however, after critical examination of all methods only the arithmetic developed in this simple model will be used to examine three methods used in evaluating capital budget proposals: (1) cash payback, (2) net present value, (3) discounted cash flow (DCF) rate of return— sometimes referred to as the "internal rate of return."

Cash payback is commonly used by businessmen evaluating investment opportunities, but it does not measure rate of return. It measures only the length of time it takes to recover the cash outlay for the investment. It indicates cash at risk. In our model there are costs of $500 committed in year 0. To determine payback we merely add the unadjusted cash flow for each year and determine how many years it takes to get the outlay back. In the first two years $450 is recovered, and by the end of the third year $600 is recovered. By interpolation we find cash recovery to be approximately 2.3 years. It is obvious that the rational businessman does not commit large sums of money just to recover it. He expects a rate of return commensurate with the risks and his alternative use of his funds in alternative investments (opportunity cost). In our example the calculation of payback reveals a relatively short exposure of funds and cash flow continuing beyond the payback period. It is interesting information in overall project evaluation, but not conclusive. Our model will automatically throw off payback as a byproduct as we calculate the crucial time-adjusted net present value of the investment and DCF rate of return.

A version of cash payback that has come on the scene recently to aid in the evaluation of ultra-high-risk investments is described as the cash bailout method. This approach takes into account not only the annual cash flow as shown in Table 2, but also the estimated liquidation value of the assets at the end of each year. If the liquidation value of a highly specialized project is zero, then cash payback and cash bailout are the same. But if it is assumed in our example that the liquidation value of the investment at the end of year 1 will be $275, the cash bailout would be one year (cash flow $225 plus liquidation value $275 = $500 original cash commitment).

We consider net present value as described a valid basis for determining the economic consequence of an investment decision. Many business economists use it as their sole criterion for the go, no-go decision for investment. We recognize this method as paramount throughout our analysis but prefer using it in conjunction with other measures rather than as the sole criterion.

Arithmetic and Concept of Discounted Cash Flow Rate of Return

We are now ready to examine the concept of DCF-ROR. It is completely different from the return on investment (ROI) commonly used by businessmen. The conventional ROI is computed for an accounting period, generally on the accrual book figure; investment is taken at original cost although it is sometimes taken at half original cost; no adjustment is made for time value when looked at in the long run.

We are talking about a very different rate of return on investment. The discounted cash flow rate of return in the interest rate that discounts a project's net cash flow to zero present value. Let us expand Table 2, which shows a $60 NPV when a discount factor of 10 percent is used, to Table 3, which adds a discount factor of 18 percent and yields a $0 NPV.

The DCF rate of return is 18 percent. By definition the DCF-ROR is the rate of return on the project determined by finding the interest rate at which the sum of the stream of after-tax cash flows, discounted to present worth, equals the cost of the project. Or, stated another way, the rate of return is

Table 3. Arithmetic of determining DCF rate of return.

YEAR	CASH FLOW	PV OF $1 @ 10%	DISCOUNTED CASH FLOW	PV OF $1 @ 18%	DISCOUNTED CASH FLOW
0	$(500)	1.000	$(500)	1.000	$(500)
0–1	225	.952	214	.915	206
1–2	225	.861	194	.764	172
2–3	150	.779	117	.639	96
3–4	50	.705	35	.533	26
Total	$150		$60 NPV		$0 NPV

the maximum constant rate of interest the project could pay on the investment and break even. How was the 18 percent determined? By trial and error.

There are many analysts who use the net present value method exclusively; some use the DCF rate of return; others use the two methods to complement each other. Using NPV, positive or negative dollar values are determined with the cost of capital as the bench mark. Excess dollar PV is evaluated and a judgment is made. The DCF rate of return approach ignores the cost of capital in calculation and determines what the rate of return is on the total cash flow. The result of this approach on our example is to convert the $60 NPV into a percentage. It works out to 8 percent on top of the 10 percent that had been calculated for the NPV. Many businessmen prefer working with the single figure of 18 percent for evaluating a project against a known cost of capital, instead of describing a project as having an NPV of $60 over the cost of capital. It is our feeling that the two methods complement each other, and under certain circumstances one may give a better picture than the other.

Let us reexamine this special DCF rate of return to see what distinguishes it from the conventional rate of return. It is time-adjusted to base year 0, so that all dollars are on a common denominator basis; it is calculated absolutely on a cash flow basis; the investment is a definite time-adjusted value; the rate of return is determined at a single average rate over the total life of the investment. Certain implications of this statement require explanation.

The DCF rate of return is calculated over the full life of the project and the accountant's yearly ROI cannot be used to test the success/failure of the new investment. If the planned life of a project is 10 years, and if it can be segregated from other facets of the operation, the DCF rate of return has meaning only when the full economic life of the project is completed. However, in this case it is possible to monitor results on a year-to-year basis by examining the actual dollar cash flow and comparing it with the projected cash flow. (Observe the assumption that the project is separate and distinct from the rest of the operation.)

The one thing that disturbs businessmen most with the DCF rate of return concept is the underlying mathematical assumption that all cash flows are reinvested immediately and constantly at the same rate as that which yields a net present value of 0. In our example in Table 3, 18 percent was used as the discount factor as a constant. Another case could just as easily have indicated a 35 percent rate of return, with the implicit assumption that the cash flow was reinvested at 35 percent. But if the earning experience indicates a cost of capital of 10 percent, how can we reconcile the assumption that we can continue to earn 35 percent on the incremental flow?

Even though a firm's average earnings reflect a cost of capital of 10 percent, the demands on incremental new investment may well have to be 18 to 35 percent to compensate for investments that fail to realize projected earnings. As long as opportunities are available to invest at an indicated 18 percent or 35 percent, it does not follow automatically that it is inconsistent with the average earnings of 10 percent. However, if it is felt that a projected rate of return of 18 percent, in our example, is a once-in-a-lifetime windfall and no new opportunities can be found to exceed the average 10 percent rate, then we are in trouble with our DCF rate of return concept. The reinvestment rate will not stand up. In this situation we have to combine both net present value and rate of return to explain the situation in this way: the 10 percent rate of return of this project covers the opportunity cost of money and throws off an additional $60 cash flow. If other projects of the same magnitude can be found so that the total cash flow generated can be reinvested at the same rate there would actually be a rate of return on the project of 18 percent (the DCF rate of return). The lack of other good investment opportunities is a constraint on the full earning capacity of the project.

We have examined three methods of evaluating investment opportunities. Cash payback evaluates money at risk. Present value measures the ability to cover the opportunity cost of an investment on a time-adjusted basis of money and indicates by a net present value whether the project under consideration will yield a "profit" or a "loss." The discounted cash flow rate of return is an extension of the net present value concept and translates it into a single rate of return that when compared with the opportunity cost of capital gives a valid basis for evaluation.

Since NPV and DCF-ROR concepts take into account the opportunity cost of capital through the discounting technique, it may be stated as a principle that all projects under consideration where this opportunity cost is covered should be accepted. This proposition is both theoretically and practically sound, but three factors need to be considered: How do you determine the minimum acceptable rate of return (the opportunity cost of capital) to select the proper discounting factor? How can you assume no constraints on the supply of capital so that all worthwhile projects can be accepted? How do you take risk into account when examining indicated results? These questions will be examined in the next three sections.

Minimum Acceptable Rate of Return— Cost of Capital

How do you determine the minimum acceptable rate of return (cost of capital) used in discounting? Again a caution: The cost of capital concept used here is not the same as the cost of borrowing. This is probably the most critical factor in the evaluation process. It is a unique and personal rate to each company. There is no guide to look to in other firms. Two firms looking at a potential investment, say an acquisition, may place two completely different values on it. To Company A, with a minimum required rate of return of 10 percent, the investment could be attractive, while to Company B, with a required rate of return of 25 percent, the investment would be totally unacceptable. The difference is centered in the cost of capital to each firm, its opportunity rate of return—the rate that can be expected on alternative investments having similar risk characteristics. An example of the arithmetic involved in reaching this conclusion can be seen when we modify Table 2 to include both a 10 percent and 25 percent discount factor and assume that both companies A and B are the potential sole bidders for an investment with an asked price of $500 and a net cash flow of $150. (See Table 4.)

Table 4. Comparison of NPV using 10% and 25% discount factors.

YEAR	CASH FLOW	(A) PV OF $1 @ 10%	DISCOUNTED CASH FLOW	(B) PV OF $1 @ 25%	DISCOUNTED CASH FLOW
0	$(500)	1.000	$(500)	1.000	$(500)
1	225	.952	214	.885	199
2	225	.861	194	.689	155
3	150	.779	117	.537	81
4	50	.705	35	.418	21
Total	$150		$60 NPV		$(44) NPV

The investment is very attractive to Company A but completely unacceptable to Company B—it would realize less than its objective of 25 percent. If Company A were in a position to know the cost of capital of Company B it would know that Company B would not bid at all for this investment. Company A would know that it would be the sole bidder.

If a company has successfully earned 25 percent on the capital employed in the firm, an investment opportunity to be attractive would have to yield at least that rate. The 25 percent represents the cost of capital to that firm and an investment opportunity offering only 15 percent would be rejected. A second firm with a 10 percent cost of capital would find the same 15 percent potential attractive and accept it. Thus the same 15 percent opportunity investment is attractive to one and unattractive to the other. Both firms analyzing the identical situation reach different logical conclusions.

Cost of capital in our analysis is *always* considered to be the combined cost of equity capital and permanent debt. We evaluate economic success/failure of a project without regard to how it is financed. Yet we know that money available for investment is basically derived from two sources: debt with its built-in tax saving so that its cost is half the market price for money (assuming a 50 percent tax rate), and equity, which has as its cost the opportunity cost of capital of the owners.

It is necessary at times to break down the combined cost of capital into its components of cost of debt capital and cost of equity capital to put it in terms understandable to the businessman who commonly measures results in terms of return on equity. To illustrate this cost of capital concept, we will assume that a corporation is owned by a single individual whose investment objectives are clearly defined. The total capitalization of the firm is $100, made up of $30 permanent debt capital and $70 owner's equity capital. If preferred stock was outstanding at a fixed cost it would be treated the same as debt. The after-tax interest rate of the debt money is 2.75 percent. The after-tax dollar return on the combined debt and equity capital of $100 under various operations would appear as shown in Table 5.

Restating these dollars as rates of return on the investment of $100, $30 debt and $70 equity, the percentage return on capital would be as shown in Table 6.

If the company has been earning an average of $10 on the total investment of $100, and the cost of debt is $.825, the earnings on owner's equity is $9.175. Stated as a rate of return,

Table 5. After-tax dollar income on investment of $100.

INCOME ON TOTAL INVESTMENT (BEFORE INTEREST)	$30 DEBT × 2.75% COST OF DEBT CAPITAL	$70 EQUITY INCOME ON OWNER'S EQUITY
$ 8.00	$0.825	$ 7.175
9.00	0.825	8.175
10.00	0.825	9.175
11.00	0.825	10.175
12.00	0.825	11.175

Table 6. After-tax rate of return on investment of $100.

RATE OF RETURN	COST OF DEBT CAPITAL	RATE OF RETURN ON OWNER'S EQUITY
8%	2.75% ($0.825 ÷ $30)	10.25% ($7.175 ÷ $70)
9%	2.75%	11.68%
10%	2.75%	13.11%
11%	2.75%	14.54%
12%	2.75%	15.96%

the $10 earned on $100 is 10 percent return on the total investment (combined cost of capital), and because of the leverage built into the capital structure with long-term debt, the $9.175 earnings on equity yields a return on equity of 13.11 percent (cost of equity capital). When there is a 30 percent debt structure and the average cost of debt is 2.75 percent after taxes we can readily convert return on total investment into return on equity by reading our table. It is quite simple to create similar tables for each company and its debt/equity ratio (e.g., with a 50/50 ratio and debt cost of 2.75 percent, a 10 percent return on total investment yields a 17.45 percent on equity capital). If there is the opportunity to invest the company funds in alternative situations, or reinvest the funds in the business and continue to earn at least 10 percent on the combined debt/equity funds we would describe this as the opportunity cost of capital. This is the critical rate used in discounting: the discount rate used to determine net present value and the bench mark for comparing discounted cash flow rate of return are based solely on the combined cost of capital. The rate of return to the stockholder can be derived and compared with his opportunity cost; that is, his ability to invest his funds elsewhere and earn at least the same rate.

Having decided that return on combined capital is the appropriate criterion for evaluating investment, it is necessary to follow through with this concept when projecting revenues, expenses, and net benefits. If we are to determine net benefits (cash flow) on combined capital, all charges against that capital must be excluded from the expense projections. If interest were charged in the projection, there would be double charging. This is not a novel method; it is used regularly by investment analysts who often determine income before interest on funded debt and before taxes.

As noted, interest expense on long-term debt is not included in the current expense projection because it is covered in the combined cost of capital computation. The interest on short-term debt may be a direct charge to operations if its cost is not in the invested capital base. If the major financing is handled through equity and long-term debt and the short-term borrowing is negligible, this method is acceptable. However, many companies live off their current borrowings and the short-term debt is actually part of the permanent capital. The true leverage would then be reflected in the return on owner's equity when compared with the return on total investment. Again a caution: When this method is used, the interest expense on current debt must be excluded from projected costs.

The capital funds of a company constitute a pool of monies for all projects. A particular borrowing rate for additional capital, at a time when a new project is introduced, becomes part of the pool of funds and it becomes part of the average cost of debt relative to total capital. With the addition of new funds it is the average long-run cost that is significant and not the current borrowing rate. The relevant comparison of the projected rate of return is with the average rate for the pool of funds and not the cost of the incremental funds.

In the case of the individual ownership of a corporation, the historical earnings rate can be determined along these lines and a cost of capital for opportunity cost evaluation can become a valid bench mark. If average earnings rise from $10 to $12 there is a new cost of capital, a new cutoff rate for accepting or rejecting projects. This does not imply constantly changing cutoff rates. Some years will be more profitable than other years, some years the cost of debt may be higher or lower than other years, but the earnings of the company are the average adjusted for trend. There is not much logic in setting a cutoff rate at 25 percent when the average is 10 percent just because there was once an isolated year that had unusually high earnings. Many good projects would be rejected because of an unrealistically high cutoff point. The reference point should be actual accomplishment and reasonable expectations, not wishful thinking.

When the assumption of the individual ownership of a corporation is abandoned in favor of a public corporation with a myriad of stockholders, the cost of capital concept gets into difficulty. It is difficult enough postulating the opportunity cost of capital for even a small family, but when we try to postulate the investment objectives of all the different stockholders in a large corporation things become really complex. One stockholder wants cash dividends; another wants growth and reinvestment of earnings; still another wants fast capital appreciation. The opportunity cost of capital to each owner becomes indistinguishable. We are not going to grapple with the problem of cost of capital for publicly owned corporations here because it is a problem that is extremely complex and can be highly theoretical. It is sufficient to note that some large public corporations have been able to develop a cost of capital for their capital budgeting evaluations with some success. Other public corporations have conceded that they cannot develop a cost of capital for all their stockholders and have resorted to a cutoff rate commensurate with their earnings experience. This latter approach violates the opportunity cost concept for the individual owners, but practical considerations have made it necessary to recognize the opportunity cost of the corporation as a person with only minor reference to the real persons who own the firm.

Constraints on Supply of Capital

How can you assume no constraints on supply of capital for investment? Theoretically, if the earnings of a corporation are great enough, and growing fast enough, there is no limit on the amount of debt and equity available. In good basic economic theory, firms should continue their capital expansion until the marginal cost of capital equals its marginal revenue; or stated simply, it is worth borrowing as long as the earnings exceed the cost by even a small amount. The principal limit on debt to the successful corporation becomes the ability of the management to live with it—at what point do the managers start losing sleep because they are so heavily leveraged? However, there are other practical constraints. General business conditions and the state of optimism/pessimism may lead to a limit on the amount of capital a management is willing to commit. There are constraints on the amount of risk a management may be willing to assume; there may be limits on the ability of an organization to handle certain ventures. There are probably other constraints, real and imaginary. In the budgeting process all categories of investments must be classified and weighed. The degree of risk willing to be assumed, and a commensurate return, is something that exists only in the mind of individual managements.

There is no nice formula that can set this. Depending on the management's philosophy, and assuming constraints on availability of capital, the selection may result in the rejection of good safe investments promising a 10 percent return, and acceptance of promotional investments with a great risk promising a 60 percent return, and vice versa. Another constraint mentioned is organization, which may be the decisive factor in choosing between an investment that will make few demands on management and one that will make great demands on management. The latter may offer a superior projected return, yet it may be rejected, reluctantly, because management does not have confidence in its ability to cope with it even though the indicated economic rewards are greater. The practical problems of project selections are varied and complex. While the techniques discussed are hardly the *sine qua non,* they do lend objectivity and direction.

Describing Risk and Uncertainty

How do you account for risk in evaluating the net present value or DCF rate of return? A more accurate term is uncertainty, but risk and uncertainty tend to be used interchangeably by businessmen. The technical difference between the two terms is found in the ability to determine probability of future outcome. Risk, with respect to outcome, implies that future events can be determined within a range of known probabilities, while uncertainty implies that probabilities of outcome cannot be established. Not all proposals have exactly the same element of risk. One investment risk category, the outlay of funds to introduce labor-saving equipment, can be evaluated quite accurately; the projected benefits may be almost a certainty.

Management could even decide to accept all such proposals where indicated NPV exceeds the combined cost of capital. Another category of risk may be the introduction of new product lines. The difference in uncertainty between the two categories is obvious. There probably would be no blanket acceptance of proposals for new products at the cost of capital cutoff rate.

The discount factor remains constant no matter what the

risk. The recognition of the different risk categories results in a subjective evaluation of the uncertainties of the venture and a markup on the cost of capital for the go, no-go decision. For example, with a cost of capital of 10 percent, a proposal is made to invest in replacement equipment. There is a modest NPV, little uncertainty. All such proposals would be segregated and acted upon and probably accepted. The second situation, introducing a completely new line or lines whose success is highly uncertain and producing a modest positive NPV, would hardly be acceptable. All such risky proposals would be segregated and judged individually within this special group. To compensate for the uncertainty, a minimum acceptable cutoff rate may be two or three times the cost of capital rate. Average success/failure may actually fall to the 10 percent average cost of capital to the firm.

The determination of the projected rate of return on an investment from the NPV can be arrived at by raising the discount rate until the NPV is zero. This is the DCF rate of return, which is the projected average return on the investment. If such a rate came to 18 percent against a cost of capital of 10 percent, it is still left to the judgment of management whether the additional 8 percent rate of return is adequate to cover the uncertainty of success/failure. This is how risk is usually evaluated—purely subjectively.

There are more exact and sophisticated methods that we will describe. Risk implies probabilities of success/failure. The fact that the project evaluation method we describe here is quite precise and yields a definite answer must not blind us to the reality that decisions are always made in the face of uncertainty. The rate of return description of a project's economic consequences is a single, uncertain prediction of projected revenues and expenses. We cannot ever completely remove this uncertainty. The best we can do is to describe the probable range and intensity of uncertainty involved and the economic consequences of forecasting errors. Next, we briefly discuss three methods that have been found helpful in performing this work.

Sensitivity Analysis

Sensitivity analysis seeks to determine how much a project's net present value or DCF rate of return will be affected (its "sensitivity") when a single factor, or specific group of factors, changes by a given amount. Let's say that for a given project we have been able to predict the volume of product sales with relative certainty, but the price forecast remains very doubtful. To make a sensitivity analysis we would repeat the evaluation using different prices; this would show how much the NPV changes with each price change.

When used with discretion, the results of sensitivity analyses are helpful in estimating the economic consequences of specific forecasting errors. As a minimum requirement, each project evaluation should describe the effect of a wrong forecast in the factor or factors judged most uncertain. However, with analysis of this type we are measuring the effect of change of a single factor or groups of factors while all other factors in the projection are held constant. When other components of the projection change, and they are ignored, the new answers may have serious limitations. For example, to change projected prices but to hold volume and costs constant may be unrealistic. We become "practical" at this point and settle for simple sensitivity analysis and get rough answers because manually reworking the model to reflect all possible changes in the figures to determine new cash flows becomes an almost impossible task. In this area computer programs really become significant. Hundreds of single factors can be tested against all other factors and the arithmetic can be worked accurately in minutes instead of in weeks.

Probability Adjustment

Probability is the preferred method of organizing estimates of both the range and intensity of uncertainty for the decision maker. In using this method the decision maker computes a reasonable range of possible outcomes for the economic model from very unfavorable to very favorable. He then estimates in his own mind the probability that each will occur. If the unfavorable outcome seems more probable than the favorable one the project is probably unwise, and vice versa.

An example of probability analysis after the initial projection has been made can be prepared as a test of its validity. No one can forecast with complete confidence and certainty the annual cash flows resulting from projected volume, prices, or even costs. The probability of achievement can be examined by preparing a table of possible deviations from the forecast. Assuming the initial annual cash flows had been projected at $10,000, a reappraisal by management might indicate the following possible results:

> 5 chances in 100 annual cash flow will be $14,000
> 25 chances in 100 annual cash flow will be   12,000
> 45 chances in 100 annual cash flow will be   10,000
> 20 chances in 100 annual cash flow will be   8,000
> 5 chances in 100 annual cash flow will be   0

It is apparent that the projected $10,000 annual cash flow has been reassessed as being the most probable, and that there is also an indication that there is a 30 percent chance that it will be exceeded. However, there is a 20 percent chance that it will be less, and a 5 percent chance it will fail completely.

There is no precise formula for testing the validity of the judgments that lead to predictions of chances of success/failure. They are based upon subjective judgments of experienced and responsible executives. If this type of analysis does nothing more than force an orderly reappraisal of a project it will serve its purpose. In this example, the conclusion may be that the $10,000 annual cash flow forecast looks reasonable and the initial projection would be allowed to stand. If on the other hand the probabilities of achieving less than the $10,000 had been greater, it would probably lead to a write-down of the cash flows.

The introduction of probability analysis also opens the way to very sophisticated statistical analysis of projected results. Computer programs have been developed that measure probabilities of success/failure of the principal factors making up the projection (volume, prices, costs, etc.), and it is possible to determine projected results taking into account any combination of favorable and unfavorable events. The DCF rate of return is then stated as rates over a range of probabilities. This approach may be extremely beneficial in evaluating major projects, but one must bear in mind that the mathematics is still based on human judgments of chances of success/failure.

DECISION TREE ANALYSIS

Some large projects present a wide variety of alternatives with varying degrees of uncertainty. In such cases it may be helpful to clarify the choices, risks, cash flows, and information needs involved by developing a decision tree analysis. This analysis does not require any new measurements. The physical act of preparing a decision tree can, however, force the recognition of alternatives and possible ramifications of a decision that otherwise might not be seen. A simple decision tree is shown on the facing page.

The choice confronting the project sponsor in this analysis is to build a small plant or a large plant. He must evaluate the probabilities of high demand or low demand and the consequences of each with the alternative plants. If a small plant is built and volume develops, a second decision becomes critical: expand or don't expand. The evaluation of these alternatives and the calculation of their economic consequences is facilitated when constructed along these lines.

Project Evaluation

Evaluating components of an investment program for a firm is complex at any time. There are many categories of investments: (a) revenue-producing projects, (b) supporting

Decision Tree

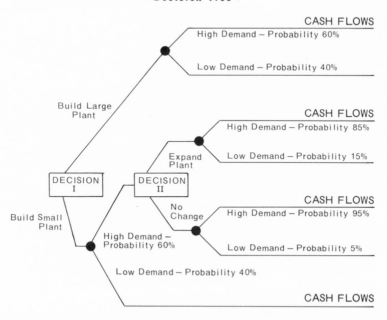

facilities projects, (c) supporting services projects, (d) cost-savings projects, and (e) last but hardly least, in this era of air and water pollution control, investment required by public authority that will yield no return. Each must be evaluated to determine its incremental consequence.

When a project is isolated from the rest of the operation, evaluation is relatively clear. But sometimes a planned major investment embraces several auxiliary projects which, evaluated by themselves, are not very meaningful. When this occurs, it is necessary to construct a master model that includes all of the projects. Some of the auxiliary projects may not come into being for several years after the main investment is made, and may or may not produce a net positive cash flow. The master model in simple form may take on the appearance shown in Table 7 if individual projects of the types (a), (b), (c)

Table 7. Master project.

PROJECT	NPV	0	1	2	3	4	5	- - -	15
(a)	100	(30)	(2)	14	14	13	13		40
(b)	40	—	—	(15)	5	5	5		20
(c)	(26)	—	(2)	(2)	(4)	(4)	(4)		(10)
Total	114	(30)	(4)	(3)	15	14	14		(50)

above are assumed (the figures do not add up—only format is demonstrated).

If the three projects are interrelated they should be projected as a single entity. In our example, (a) is assumed to be a major facility that to be successful needs (b) added in three years as supporting facilities; (b) would have no basis for existence if (a) were not created. Project (c) may possibly be identified as a new computer/information system that will produce only costs, but would not exist if (a) and (b) were not created. All costs and all benefits for all corollary investments need to be projected as far into the future as possible to get a true evaluation. Investment evaluations that are made of a project with all the certainty of a DCF percentage can be grossly misleading if the supporting investment of satellites is not taken into account. Actually, these are not separate investments. There is only one—(Project abc). The evaluation has to be of the new single entity. The post audit can be of only the conglomerate single entity (abc).

Projects of the cost-savings category (d) are generally easiest to identify and evaluate. There are relatively clear-cut choices: Invest $40,000 today for new labor-saving machines that will reduce labor costs $12,000 per year; the machines will last eight years, and quality of performance will be unchanged. Determine the NPV and/or DCF rate of return and accept/ reject. Such investment opportunities constantly arise, but it is almost impossible to project them as part of a master project. As a result, such investments are evaluated as isolated investment opportunities that may occur in three years, or eight years, or never. When they occur, if of major proportions, they affect the potential return on the total investment.

A cost-incurring project (e), such as spend $100,000 to prevent air pollution or be closed up, is one of the few black-and-white decisions a businessman faces. He decides to go on. Ideally he would expense it. He may have to capitalize it and write it off, and in addition have annual related operating expenses. This nondiscretionary investment falls into the same general category as type (c), support project. The cash flow is always negative and must be included as an integral part of the master investment. If the commitment is large enough it may sharply reduce the original projection and a revision may be necessary.

Selecting Among Projects

Based upon the techniques for evaluating planned capital investment, it is now possible to move to the methods of selecting among projects. As noted above, in theory, selecting among projects is easy. Invest in anything that when discounted at the appropriate marginal rate will yield a positive NPV. Practically, for many reasons, there are constraints on capital in the minds of most managers. Let us look at the project selection problems that are involved for projects under consideration in a particular risk category when there is a limit on capital.

We have selected the NPV method as the best approach to analyze proposed projects of varying lives. Comparing projects under the DCF-ROR method can be misleading because of the different life factor and the reinvestment factor inherent in each ROR. Excess NPV avoids this difficulty. When the various projects are converted into a profitability index, selection is further facilitated. The profitability index is the ratio of the NPV to investment. For example:

$$\frac{\text{Present value of expected benefits}}{\text{Investment}} = \frac{\$132,000}{\$100,000} = 1.32$$

In selecting projects when a limit is imposed upon the amount available for investment, we look for the combination that will maximize combined net present value without exceeding the imposed limit. We know that we have reached this goal when we can no longer increase the combined net present value by substituting one project for another and still satisfy the constraint.

A way to achieve a satisfactory combination of projects is through trial and error. As a guide we can use the profitability index (see Table 8). However, such ratios are not foolproof. This is illustrated where there are three possible projects requiring a total of $1,500 in initial outlays, but where $1,000 is the imposed limit.

Table 8. Profitability index.

	NET PRESENT VALUE		INVESTMENT: CASH OUTLAY		PROFIT-ABILITY INDEX
Project A	$1,000	÷	$600	=	1.67
Project B	700	÷	500	=	1.40
Project C	500	÷	400	=	1.25

The choice is investment in A + C (cash outlay $1,000) and B + C (cash outlay $900). Since A + C have a combined greater NPV than B + C ($1,500 vs. $1,200), A + C should be selected even though C's ratio (1.25) is less than B's ratio (1.40). Such differences are common. The profitability index must always be used judiciously. When there are numerous projects to choose among, the combining process becomes more difficult.

Summary

After examining working concepts of what is involved in the capital budgeting process, the reader can appreciate the many problems that must be resolved when attempting to be "objective" and "scientific" in his capital commitments. The first step is planning the new investment. This is critical. Investments with long life expectancy are wrapped in a shroud of uncertainty, yet plans and projections based on intuition and a minimum of facts are often made with an aplomb that gives the impression of certainty. Hard conclusions and decisions are often reached based on very soft facts. The recognition of uncertainty and its proper evaluation is probably the most important step in the analysis of an investment. Yet this is the area where we often become "practical" because the task is so difficult both in the gathering of the necessary data and its evaluation. If all the sophisticated measures of evaluating uncertainty are attempted manually, the paperwork literally becomes overwhelming and it becomes advisable to turn to computer programs for help with the mathematics.

The use of the computer is becoming accepted practice in the capital budgeting procedure. The description of the manual methods of computation already described, and those that follow in the model, assume an aura of certainty. Every attempt is made to approximate the greatest probability of certainty, yet the calculations that evolve from a single measure must be evaluated in the light of uncertainty. The computer programs based upon sensitivity analysis, decision tree analysis, and probability analysis that have been mentioned can now extend our computational abilities.

A program based on a technique known as "Monte Carlo Simulation" makes possible the "simulation" of future events by sampling values from our estimates under favorable and unfavorable circumstances and making all necessary cash flow calculations by random chance. This is an important step forward in the sophisticated handling of uncertainty based upon the principles we have very briefly examined. Suffice it to state at this juncture that where computational speed and accuracy are beneficial, computer programs based upon sound theory and principles exist or are being developed. Our primer has recited the principles on which programs have been developed and can be employed advantageously in many situations.

After the development of a plan on an incremental basis, we spent a good deal of time developing and examining recommended criteria for evaluating projected investments. A simple two-step model was developed. The first step, with three elements, is applicable in all situations:

Benefits less Costs = Cash Flow

This is the basis for preparing all projections. The next step is to adjust the cash flow to eliminate time differences. All cash flows are adjusted to year "zero," which becomes the common denominator for evaluations. The adjustment is made by discounting future values to present values. The mechanics of discounting are not difficult to master but the determination of a discount factor is. The discount factor is the interest rate that equates with the firm's combined cost of capital. This is a relatively new concept and should not be confused with the traditional cost of borrowing. Cost of capital is the rate earned on the combined capital of equity holders plus the permanent debt used as part of the capital of the firm. This simple explanation stands up for the firm with a sole owner who can evaluate the rate of return with his own opportunity cost of capital. When a public corporation becomes involved, the calculation of equity cost of capital could become extremely complex if an attempt were made to take into account the opportunity costs of the various stockholders. For our examination we have simplified the problem by recognizing a combined cost of capital where opportunity costs can be determined. This rate becomes the discount value and is used for discounting.

When proposed investment benefits are discounted at a rate consistent with cost of capital, we have a net present value that tells us that the project will yield more or less than the cost of capital. This rate becomes our cutoff rate when considering accept/reject. Many analysts use this NPV as the sole criterion for evaluation of the project. We recognize the importance of NPV but carry it a step further to discounted cash flow rate of return (DCF-ROR) because the latter changes the excess NPV dollars to a single percentage rate of return that is often easier to comprehend. These two measuring devices that are time-adjusted through the discounting methodology are teamed up with several other criteria to bring the maximum information to bear on the analysis. The most prominent of these is cash payback, which is introduced to reflect money at risk only, and not a rate of return. All these calculations were built on judgments by responsible executives. The final calculations are presented to a budget committee for its appraisal of the facts. The validity of the mathematics used in the projecting and final evaluation are dependent on the skill, objectivity, and integrity of the men making the multitude of subjective judgments that are needed at many stages in the development of the projection.

When an NPV or DCF-ROR is determined for a project and, if the company's alternative to investment is to do nothing, the choice is clear. When the choice of capital commitment is among several projects and there is a limit on the amount of capital available for investment, we have chosen to compare projects using NPV rather than the DCF-ROR. We are not committed to saying NPV is better than DCF-ROR in all situations, or vice versa. Each has features that work better in some situations.

We recognize the need to control authorized cash expenditures once a commitment is made. Projections of NPV or rate of return are made. If cash expenditures exceed estimates the projected benefits are meaningless. Practically, this has been a pitfall for many good capital budgeting procedures. If large overexpenditures are made, a new projection should be prepared; however, this only yields a new rate of return after the fact. By that time we are merely generating statistics.

Post audit of investment is difficult. It is often neglected. If a plan of post audit is not determined and agreed upon at the time a commitment is to be made, the probabilities are there won't be one or a post audit will be attempted and it may not be satisfactory. As all investments are projected on an incremental basis, and the results are usually part of a larger investment, there is an inability to sort out the results of the incremental portion and identify its NPV or DCF-ROR. It is not fair to management, and it is poor budgeting procedure, to establish a value upon which important decisions are made and then announce you cannot compare the results with the budget. NPV

and DCF-ROR indicate expected results over the complete life
of the investment, but there is a desire and need to appraise
results on an annual basis. For those investments that can be
identified apart from other investments, the post audit can be
in the form of tests of cash flow and adjusted financial statements. When the investment becomes an integral part of existing investments, the incremental portion cannot be identified
and plans must be made to post audit on the basis of the new
combined investment. This will involve the preparation of a
"master" investment projection at the time the incremental
investment is planned. A financial model should be prepared,
combined cash flows can be computed if desired, post audit
can be performed for the master investment. It is important
that this step be taken or the failure of post audit is almost a
certainty.

Index